The Celts

The Celts

Text by **Georges Dottin**

Translated by David Macrae

Minerva

Readers who wish to study the subject of this book in greater depth should read the major work by Georges Dottin entitled *Manuel pour servir à l'étude de l'Antiquité Celtique* (published by Honoré Champion, Paris), which contains a thorough, annotated account of all aspects of the Celts, complete with references.

© Editions Minerva, S.A., Genève, 1977
Printer industria gráfica sa
Tuset, 19   Barcelona
Sant Vicenç dels Horts 1977
Depósito legal B. 18001-1977
Printed in Spain

1. A PORTRAIT OF THE CELTS.

The first Celts seen by the Greeks and Romans in Gaul impressed them as men of gigantic stature, their hair swept up on top of their head, yet of delicate complexion. They were extremely impetuous, and tired quickly. In fact, all the barbarians of north-west Europe—Cimbrians, Germans and Sueves—were seen in these traditional terms. It is only in the writings of Virgil that one finds references to the golden hair and the milk-white necks of the Gauls who took Rome. Blond hair and a fair complexion were most often associated with the Germans and the Belgians. The men described by Diodorus as having a large stature, with soft flesh, white skin and naturally blond hair—the color of which was further enhanced by the use of a lime wash—were Galatians, or what he might have regarded as Germans. Strabo noted that the Germans were even bigger and fairer than the Gauls, while the Bretons were bigger, softer and less fair than the Gauls, but were not very well built. The Gauls were taller than the Roman soldiers, and it seems certain that the Germans, for their part, were bigger again. When Caligula, embarrassed by the small number of his captives, sought to augment them by passing off Gauls as Germans, he chose the biggest men, and had them let their hair grow long and dye it red. In the opinion of Tacitus, the fact that the hair of the Caledonians was bright red proved their Germanic origin. The Gauls, then, seem to have been quite tall, though less so than the

Celtic idol from the beginning of the Gallo-Roman period (Museum of Saint-Germain-en-Laye).

Germans; moreover, there seems to have been a preponderance of blond hair, particularly among the Gaulish tribes related to the Germans. As for the blue eyes which Tacitus and Plutarch associated with the Germans, it cannot be proved that they were a trait of the Celtic type.

The skeletons found in the tombs of the Marne, most probably of Celts, are quite short. Their average size is about 5'6½". A higher average was found at Vindelicia: 5'8". However, judging by the cephalic index of the skulls found in the tombs which are commonly thought of as Celtic, in Champagne, at Halstatt in Bavaria, the Celts were for the most part dolichocephalic. In the Tène most of the skulls have a medium cephalic index. The insular Celts from the Bronze Age are generally brachycephalic, and those of the Iron Age dolichocephalic. Since it is likely that the warriors whose remains have been found were the chiefs, one may legitimately wonder whether the data assembled has any value for the population as a whole, or whether it pertains almost exclusively to the elite of each nation.

The accuracy of our physical descriptions of the Celts, though imperfect, far surpasses our knowledge of their moral and intellectual characteristics. The qualities and faults of the Celts were recorded principally by their enemies, the Romans. One should take care not to attach too much importance to naive generalisations, based on superficial observations. In any

case, the opinions of the ancients sometimes varied widely.

Whereas Livy, like Caesar, considered their religious nature as a distinctive trait of the Gauls, Cicero felt that they were quite devoid of any sense of piety and justice. Aristotle, and, later, Diodorus and Atheneus, accused the Celts of being pederasts, though the Roman authors did not associate them with such tendencies. Polybus noted their perfidy, while Strabo found that they had a simple nature, lacking in malice, an open character with very little aptitude for guile; in his opinion, these were men who were more accustomed to fighting with their courage than through devious ruses.

One thing all the ancient authors agree on is that they were fickle and inconstant, lacking the ability to think carefully before acting. According to Polybus, Gauls tended to resolve all issues through passion rather than reason and calculating thought. Caesar was familiar with their restless, flighty nature, and their fondness for novelty; he observed that they often resolved the most important issues on the basis of rumors and reports which they never even bothered to check, and which, being for the most part specially thought up to please them, usually caused them to repent sooner or later.

Their cruelty in war had terrified the Greeks and Romans. The Celts who invaded Greece used to slaughter their prisoners and finish off the wounded where

Left: limestone torso of warrior, from Entremont, 3rd century BC. Height: 17 inches. Right: wooden votive statuette (Historical Museum, Orleans).

they lay, massacring children and old people, and raping the women. The Cisalpine and Transalpine Gauls used to chop off the heads of defeated enemies and carry them slung about their horses' necks, or stuck on the end of their lances, so as to hang them up, like trophies, outside their houses. Poşeidonios, who had seen such spectacles frequently, found that his revulsion eventually gave way to indifference.

The heads of chiefs or illustrious persons were kept in cedar oil, and were proudly displayed to visitors, though their owners would not part with them at any price. In 216 BC, the *Boii,* having killed the consul Postumius in battle, cut off his head and carried it in triumph to their most highly venerated temple, where, in keeping with custom, they gutted it and decorated it with gold, so that it could be used for ceremonial libations. There are a number of severed heads depicted on the triumphal arch at Orange, and also on a monument at Entremont, near Aix, which commemorates a victory of the Gauls over other barbarians.

Irish epics provide several examples of this savage custom. Lugaid cut off the head of Cuchulainn, Conall Cernach cut off the head of Lugaid; in one of the halls of their palace, the kings of Ulster used to keep the heads of distinguished enemies they had slain in battle.

When actually in battle, the Celts were known to have violent fits of rage; they deliberately opened up their wounds to make

them look larger, and, when defeated they often turned their weapons against themselves. At the villa Ludovisi, there is a sculpture in which a Gaul, having killed his wife, kills himself in order to avoid falling into slavery.

Their unreasoning pride even led them to fight the elements. They sometimes charged, fully armed, at the waves which threatened to flood their encampments, they would readily brave the dangers of fire and would have regarded it as an affront to their honor to run away from a collapsing wall or building. This vanity took the form of loud boasting; indeed, the authors of the ancient world attributed some famous replies to these proud warriors.

It was thought that they enrolled in expeditions to remote countries out of greed, so that they could indulge in looting, as mercenaries and nothing else. However, according to Appian, when the Roman senate offered them money if they would agree to hand over the Fabius who had committed certain common crimes, they refused to take it. The *Scordisci* would not even allow gold to enter their country.

The Celts were famous for their intemperance. It has even been argued that it was the love of wine that drew them to Italy. According to Cicero, they regarded a mixture of wine and water as poison, whereas, if one is to believe Ammianus Marcellinus, the common people used to drink themselves into a stupor which bordered on madness.

Left: the group of "severed heads", from Entremont. Height: 17 inches.
Above: double statuette (Borely Museum, Marseille).

The Celts of Gaul were most hospitable. They never locked the doors of their houses, and any passer-by could go in and share their meal with them. When strangers arrived among the Celtiberians, everyone was anxious to see them; indeed, anyone who was surrounded with visitors from outside the tribe was thought to have the special blessing of the gods. Is it right, therefore, to attribute to the Celts the custom of slaughtering strangers—a custom which, according to Diodorus, was abolished in Celtica by Herakles?

Despite the contradictions it contains, this moral portrait is certainly not very flattering for the Celts, on the whole. Those Celts who are mentioned individually by the Greek and Roman authors are presented in the most favorable light. Cicero had become a friend of the Gaulish druid Diviciacus and spoke highly of the gentleness and honesty of the Galatian king Dejotarus. The two sons of the Galatian king Adiatorix sought to outdo each other in generosity in order to see which one of them would die with their father. Clondicus, king of the Gauls, let Antigonus return unharmed after he had come to convey to the Gaulish army the perfidious proposals of Perseus, king of Macedonia. Some of the Celtic peoples were thought to have certain very sound qualities. The *Allobroges* refused to hand over to the Romans the princes of the *Salyi* who had taken refuge among them. Caesar recognized that the *Volques Tectosages*

Entrance to a Celtic citadel (Grianan of Aileach, Ireland).

enjoyed a great reputation for justice.

Ancient authors disagree quite as much about the intellectual qualities of the Celts as about their moral nature. In a famous phrase, Cato said that the Cisalpine Gauls had cultivated two arts with great talent: the art of war and the art of clever speech. Polybus, a contemporary of Cato, wrote that the Cisalpines were ignorant of everything but war and agriculture. According to Diodorus, the Transalpine Gauls were men of few words who spoke in riddles, deliberately leaving most of their meaning hidden. They were very given to hyperbole, whether in self-praise or denigration of others. Their speech was threatening, haughty and often charged with tragic overtones. However, they were intelligent and capable of learning. Yet in the opinion of Strabo those same Transalpines were fairly simple-minded and limited. Agricola found the liveliness of the Bretons preferable to the learning of the Gauls. Juvenal considered Gaul as the source from which the Bretons learnt whatever eloquence they had.

This physical, moral and intellectual portrait of the Celts tells us little that could be described as definitive; it is similar to the picture given by the Greeks and Romans of the other barbarian peoples. Even if it were accurate in every detail, it would still be impossible to conclude therefrom that the Celts were markedly different from any other people at their level of civilisation.

2. HOUSING, FOOD AND
CLOTHING.

It is in the housing, food, clothing and ornamentation of the Celts that the ancients found material for more precise observations.

According to Polybus, the peoples which settled in Cisalpine Gaul lived in scattered villages without walls. These villages were doubtless similar to the *vici* which Caesar had found in Gaul: wooden houses, which could easily be burned down and destroyed. Octodorus was one such *vicus,* large enough to accommodate eight cohorts. In the writings of Caesar, individual dwellings are known as *œdificia;* these were probably fairly large structures, surrounded by wood, or farm buildings used to house livestock, farmers or crops.

Gaulish houses were usually thatched and dome-like, being built of planks and willow supports. Some had an outer facing of mud, while others were covered with oak shingles or straw mixed with earth. The Bretons built very similar houses, of reeds and wood. The *Caledonii* still had neither fortified walls, nor towns, nor plowed fields, as late as the second century of the Christian era.

The houses and palaces of the Irish of the epics seem to have been circular, like the Gaulish rotunda mentioned by Strabo. The fireplace was situated in the middle. There was only one door. Beds were placed around the walls, from one side of the door to the other. The royal seat was behind the fire and in front of the door. The principal chiefs sat on either side of the king, against the wall.

In wartime the Gauls used to take refuge in the fortified camps known as *oppida* in the writings of Caesar. The *oppida* of the Bretons were nothing more than retrenched camps defended by a ditch and a mound of earth with a stockade, within which they erected temporary huts for themselves next to some sheds for their livestock.

The Belgian peoples which inhabited the Ardennes forest used to take special precautions in time of war by weaving the branches of climbing thorny bushes into a forbidding mesh of thorns, so that any invader would find all paths blocked; in certain places, they would retreat, with their families, to small islands in the midst of swamps deep inside the forest, having first driven stakes into the ground along potential paths. The *oppida* of Gaul were towns which could offer shelter to the inhabitants of neighboring areas, together with their livestock and furniture, but which also had a permanent population, among which were some merchants. There were far fewer *oppida* in Gaul than there were *vici*. The Helvetii had twelve *oppida* and four hundred *vici*. In the *oppidum* of Bratuspantium, the *Bellovaci* had succeeded in taking refuge with their women, children and all their property. At the time of the Gaulish insurrection, the *Bellovaci* promised to raise an army of ten thousand men, though it was said that they could have provided as many as a hundred thousand. The *cas-*

tella mentioned by Caesar in the same context as the *oppida* were probably small fortified points. Aduataca, the city of the Eburones, was described as such a *castellum*.

The walls of Gaulish fortifications have been described in detail by Caesar. The construction of these walls proceeded as follows: solid beams were laid out on the ground about two feet apart; they were joined by transverse struts, and the cavity thus formed was filled with earth. Large stones were used to face the front. A second layer was then added to the first, being made in exactly the same way, with the same distances between the beams, so that the stones placed between each layer supported the layer above, and so on until the desired height had been reached. These interwoven layers of stone and wood, besides being pleasing to the eye, also had major military advantages, as the stone was a protection against fire and the wood against the danger of the battering ram.

At Mont Beuvray large nails and wooden pins have been found which must have been from the ramparts of Bibractium. The combinded use of beams and stone can be seen in the ruins of the *oppidum* of Murcens (Lot). The houses discovered in the *oppidum* at Bibractium, which date from before the Roman conquest, they were built on a rectangular plan, most of them being made of clay masonry, without lime; quite a large number of them are of wood and puddlework.

Celtic remains in Wales.

16

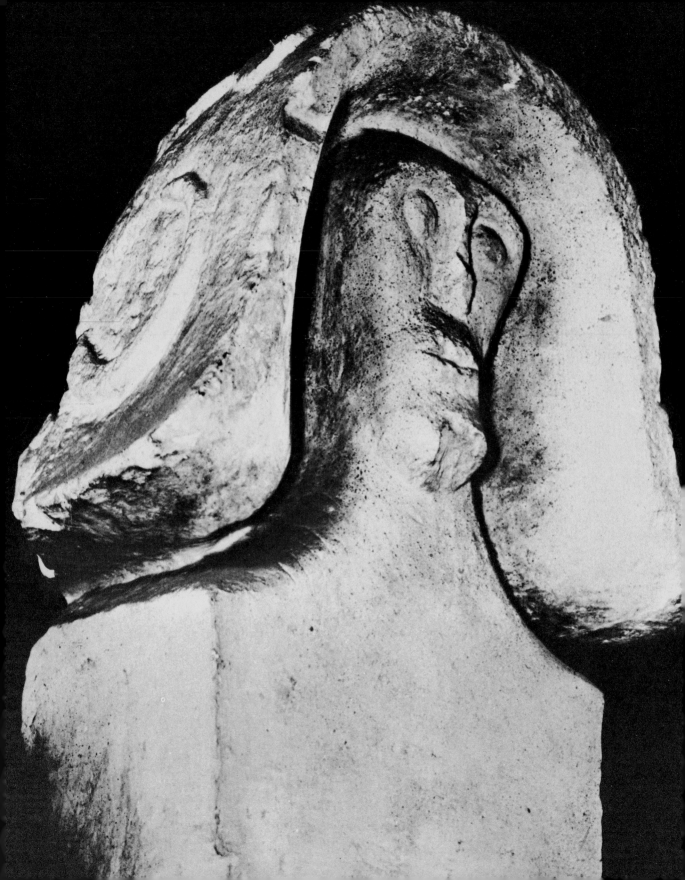

Most of them are half-underground, access being provided by a staircase, inside the building, of a few steps. The floor was of beaten earth, and the roof, most probably, was thatched. The houses had fireplaces, with andirons shaped like a ram's head, made of clay covered with mica dust.

The huge enclosures known in Ireland as *dun*—one of the most interesting of which is *dun Aengus,* at Aranmore, on Galway Bay—were built of dry stone. The walls of *Dun Aengus* take the form of three irregular circles, at the top of a cliff 300 feet high. They are 20 feet thick and from 20 to 50 feet high.

The Gauls described in the writings of Polybus were not familiar with the concept of furniture, and their only bed was grass. The Cisalpine *Boii,* according to Livy, had brass vases, the *vasa aerea Gallica* which appeared in the triumph of P. Cornelius Scipio, but it seems likely that these vases, like the *signs,* or statues, described in the same text, belonged to the fittings of the temple.

Poseidonios, quoted by Atheneus, noted that the Celts, at meal-time, used to sit on bales of hay around low circular wooden tables. They had neither forks nor spoons: they simply grabbed chunks of meat and tore them apart like lions. If they found something difficult to rip in this way, they would take out a small cutlass from a sheath at their side. Their dishes were made of silver, copper or earthenware, and they used some wicker or wooden baskets at

Figure of a warrior, from Sainte-Anastasie (Gard), France.

19

Ancient knife (Museum of Gien). Right: drawings inside a tumulus at Locmariaquer (Morbihan).

table also. Their goblets, not unlike certain Greek vases, were of earthenware or silver. Diodorus talks of Gauls sleeping on the hides of wild animals, and squatting at meal-times on wolf- or dog-hides, next to a blazing hearth, replete with cauldrons and spits roasting huge portions of meat. According to Strabo, almost all the Celts used to sleep on the ground and take their meals sitting on beds of straw, grass or leaves. He must have been referring to the period during which Poseidonios visited Gaul, because Pliny the Elder spoke of mattresses and stuffed beds as a Gaulish invention.

The Cisalpine Celts led an extremely frugal life; their main food was pork. For this reason they raised vast numbers of pigs, which the swineherds used to sum-

mon from their pastures with a blast on the trumpet. Poseidonios thought that the Gauls ate a great deal of roasted, boiled or grilled meat, and only little bread. In Pliny's opinion, Gaulish bread was very light. In the time of Strabo, the Gauls, and more particularly the *Sequani*, did a flourishing trade in salted meats. In the first century BC, Gaulish hams and dried meats were highly reputed. Pork fat served as oil. The Marseillais used millet flour and barley broth.

Dairy products were also much used among the Gauls. The remains of vast cheese-making installations have been found at Mont Beuvray. The inhabitants of the Mediterranean and Atlantic coasts lived on fish, which they seasoned with salt, vinegar and cummin. The *Caledonii* and

Left: the Skelligs, Celtic remains on the Irish coast.
Above: terra cotta vase from Grobbendonk (Copenhagen).

the *Maeatae,* on the other hand, made no use at all in their diet of the abundant stocks of fish in the waters of their region. For their daily sustenance the Bretons used to shell the oldest ears of cereal in their barns. Some of their tribes were lacking in industry that, although they had an abundance of milk, they never made cheese from it. Others lived off bark and roots, and had devised a type of food which was so filling that a small amount, the size of a bean, was enough to assuage the pangs of hunger completely.

About the time of Poseidonios, the standard drink of the Gauls was a beer made from grain, with or without honey. This drink, to which cumin was sometimes added, was called *corma*. The guests all drank out of the same goblet, which the servant passed around to right and to left. Diodorus spoke of two types of Gaulish drink: a barley beer and mead. The beer

was nothing more than a kind of fetid juice made from rotten barley, so the Gauls tended to prefer the wine which was brought back from Italy by merchants. Even in the 1st century BC, this wine was the drink of the rich; they would willingly swap a young boy for a barrel of wine, and then drink the wine neat until they were thoroughly drunk. Some Gauls would lie down on their shields and, in exchange for wine or money, would allow their throats to be cut, as long as the wine or the money should go to their descendants after their death. However, in Caesar's time, the *Nervii* prohibited the use of wine and the ownership of any luxury item. The Celtiberians used to drink their wine mixed with honey.

We have a fairly good idea of the way in which the Celts held their grand ceremonial dinners. The guests sat in a circle; the man who was more distinguished than all the others in terms of military prowess, birth

23

or wealth, sat in the middle of the assembled company. The master of the household sat next to him, and the others sat on either side, according to their rank. Those bearing shields were arranged behind, and those bearing lances sat in a circle at the other end of the hall, where they were served like their masters. According to Phylarch, the Galatians simply used to place the food in a disorderly fashion on the table—hunks of bread and the meat which had been cooking in the cualdrons; but no-one dared take anything for himself until he had seen the king take his portion first.

Certain Celtic meals became legendary. Luernios, the father of Bituitos, the king of the *Averni* defeated by the Romans in 121 BC, built an enclosure twelve stadiums in area and loaded it with vats of fine drinks and tables full of the best food which sufficed to feed a vast number of people for several days in a row. Ariamnes, a rich Galatian from Asia, had boasted that he would feed all the Galatians for a whole year. And he kept his word. At the most suitable points along the roads of the region he built cabins of reeds and wicker, each capable of accommodating four hundred people or more. Inside were large

Above: vase from a Celtic covered way, northern Brittany (Côtes-du-Nord).— Below: statue of a wild boar.

cauldrons filled with all sorts of cooked meats. Every day, a large number of animals were slaughtered—bulls, pigs, sheep. Barrels of wine and bowls of meal had also been prepared. Besides the Galatians themselves, who came from the fields and the villages to enjoy this spectacular largesse, any traveller who happened to be in the area was also invited to partake for himself.

Our information about Celtic dress, based on the writings of the authors of antiquity and on archeological finds, is quite full. At the battle of Telamon, between the Cisalpine Gauls and the Romans in 225 BC, whereas the *Gaesati* fought naked, the *Insubres* and the *Boii* wore breeches and light sashes. However, Polybus does not use the Gaulish word for breeches, using instead the Greek word for Persian trousers.

Diodorus gives us a complete description of the dress of the Gauls. They wore motley tunics and trousers; the striped sashes which they wore over their shoulders, and which were made of a fabric with small colored checks, were secured with a clasp. The fabric itself was light in summer and heavier in winter. The breeches worn by the Gauls are rarely shown on statues and bas-reliefs, in which the figures are nude in most cases. A bronze vase from Pompeii depicts two bearded Gauls wearing breeches, with a *torques* around their neck and carrying a long hexagonal shield in their left hand. One of the warriors from the Ammendola sarcophagus is wearing narrow breeches, as are the prisoners shown in the upper part of the bas-relief.

The breeches do not seem to be of Celtic origin. It was unknown among the ancient Gaelic tribes of Ireland and Scotland; the Narbonnaise region of what is now France was unique in that it bore the name *Gallia bracata;* the word *braka* is probably cognate with the Latin *suf-frago,* ham; if this is so, the word *braca* was borrowed by the Celts from the Germanic tribes, the *g* remaining unchanged in Celtic and becoming *k* in the Germanic tongues. Trousers were commonly worn among certain other peoples of antiquity, such as the Persians and the Scythians.

Besides the Gauls, the Ligurians, Germans, Lusitanians and Roman soldiers all wore the *sagum* as a cloak. It was made of sheep's wool. Those made of coarser, long-haired wool, were known as *lainai.* This garment in probably different from the *Linna* which Plautus describes as being woven in Gaul, and which was a square and rather soft sash. The *sagum* of the Celtiberians, according to Appian, was a sort of thick, double cloak secured by a fibula, or buckle. It was made of a fuzzy black wool not unlike the hair of the goat.

On the triumphal arch at Orange the Gauls are depicted naked, with a *sagum* draped over their shoulders. This *sagum* was attached by a buckle on the right shoulder, over the tunic. The *sagum* is also shown on the statue of the Gaul at the villa

*Left: a statuette of a runner, from the Gallo-Roman period (Historical Museum, Orleans).—
Above: Gaulish prisoners on the Triumphal Arch at Orange.*

Ludovisi and on the Ammendola sarcophagus. Large numbers of the buckles (broaches or safety pins) which were used to attach the *sagum*) have been found. They are in the shape of an arc: the pin is attached to the arc either directly, or by rings or buttons. They were extremely varied: bronze was the commonest material, followed by iron, while gold and silver were used only rarely. At Halstatt, fibulas have been found in a wide variety of shapes: semi-circular, boat-shaped, serpentine, half-moon, double disk, with a drum, and T-shaped. Those which had an S-shaped foot joined to the arc by an eyelet or a button belong to the Tène period. The more complex models are adorned with enamels or coral, while the fibulas made of iron sometimes have bronze or glass pearl ornaments.

The Gaulish tunic differed from that of the Greeks and the Romans in that it had sleeves. It did not extend beyond the upper part of the thighs and the lower back.

The Celts loved brightly colored clothes; the chiefs wore dyed fabrics with gold clasps; their striped, embroidered garments had attracted the attention of the rest of the ancient world. According to Pliny, the Gauls were the inventors of checked cloth; they had managed to extract a purple dye from the bilberry, scarlet from the hyacinth, and an assortment of colors from various other plants.

The footwear of Gaulish origin which the Romans called *gallicae*, and which came to be used in Italy shortly before the time of Cicero, was a kind of sandal not unlike the *soleae*, which left much of the upper part of the foot exposed. They were tied up with leather laces or string. Most of the warriors represented on the Ammendola sarcophagus are barefoot. Only the chief and several prisoners are wearing a thick-soled shoe, cut along the uppers.

Some Celtic tribes seem to have been quite unaware of the use of clothes. In the 2nd century AD, the inhabitants of north-

27

ern Brittany went about completely naked, and stayed in their swamps for days at a time. Generally speaking, the Gauls one sees on the monuments of antiquity are shown naked. Some Gaulish tribes are known to have been in the habit of undressing completely before going into battle.

Since there was much native gold in Gaul, the inhabitants used to collect it and use it to adorn their persons. Both men and women wore gold rings on their wrists and arms, as well as necklaces and bangles made of the precious metal. Some golden necklaces were extremely heavy. The Roman Senate gave two petty Transalpine kings two necklaces weighing five pounds each, whereas in another instance, another Transalpine king received a necklace weighing two pounds. With the necklaces of the Cisalpine Gauls, C. Flaminius was able to assemble enough gold to erect a golden trophy to Jupiter.

The Gauls are sometimes depicted with necklaces and bracelets. The dying Gaul on the Capitol is wearing a *torques* around his neck, while this same ornament is to be found on the six Gaulish warriors on the Ammendola sarcophagus. The Gaul on the monument at Montdragon has a golden ring around his arm.

Some Celts used to shave their beard completely, while others let it grow to a moderate length; however, the nobles used to shave their cheeks, while letting their moustaches grow so as to cover their mouth.

Personal hygiene among the ancient Celts cannot have been very sophisticated. However, Ammianus Marcellinus thought that the Gauls of his day were remarkably clean.

Soap made from tallow or ash was, according to Pliny, a Gaulish invention. In order to preserve the freshness of their complexion, the Celtic women used beer foam. Washing and cleaning of teeth, at least among the Celtiberians, was done with urine stored for a long time in special tanks. *Valeriana celtica* was used to prepare a perfume known as Gaulish spikenard.

Besides jewelry, the Bretons also used the tattoo as a form of personal ornament. Caesar wrote that all the Bretons used to dye their bodies with pastel, thus turning their bodies a bright blue color which made them look particularly horrible in battle. They let their hair grow long and shaved the whole of their body except the head and the upper lip. Breton women and young girls, as described by Pliny, used to dye their body with pastel, thus turning a very dark shade, for certain religious observances. Herodian and Solinus are the only authors of antiquity who associate the tattoos of the Bretons with various animals.

It has often been claimed that the relative splendor of Celtic ornamentation is evidence of an advanced stage of civilization, which contrasts sharply with the descriptions we read in the ancient authors of

Left: buckle of a swordbelt; wooden statuette of Irish origin. Below: figurine from a small Gallo-Belgian vase.

squalid dwellings and crude meals; indeed, attempts have been made to rebut the evidence of Greek and Roman observers. However, there is nothing to prove that the relationship which modern man has established between the different spheres of human activity was necessarily the same among the Celts.

3. WOMEN AND CHILDREN. DEATH.

We know little about the way of life of the Celts. With the exception of Caesar, who in any case may not have observed it very much himself, all the ancients have left us is in the form of anecdotes intended merely as illustrations for morally edifying tales.

What follows is an account of the most reliable findings of modern scholarship about the status of women and children, and customs pertaining to birth and death.

Women used to provide a dowry, but the men had to offer comparable value from their own property. The surviving spouse receives both shares, together with all gains acquired since the marriage. Husbands had absolute power over their wives. When the father of a distinguished family was on the point of death, his kin would assemble and, if there was any suspicion concerning his death, the women would be interrogated, just like the slaves. If it could be proved that their conduct had been bad, they were burnt to death and tortured. During the siege of Gergovia, the mothers tossed down clothes and money from the top of the ramparts, and, with bare breasts and outstretched arms, they begged the Romans to spare them. Some of them allowed themselves to be seized and raped by the Roman soldiers. Among the Bretons, the women belonged to ten or twelve men at a time, particularly to brothers, fathers or their children; however, the children born of such unions belonged to the

Left: Gallo-Roman bas-relief depicting Venus and a woman wearing clothes (Châtillon-sur-Seine).—Right: wooden votive offering.

man who had had the woman while she was still a virgin. In Ireland, it was thought perfectly natural for men to have sexual relations with other men's wives, mothers or sisters. Community of wives was the rule in Caledonia.

In Ireland, marriage took the form of a sale in which the father, or a relative acting on behalf of a deceased father, yielded to the bridegroom his rights over the woman being married. The value of a woman was assessed at the equivalent of three head of cattle, plus the price of honor, which varied according to the woman's social status. Besides his legitimate wife, the husband could keep several concubines in the conjugal home at the same time, if he wished. Lugaid, supreme king of Ireland, married his mother, while a king of Leinster had his two sisters as wives. Diarmait MacFergusa, the supreme king of Ireland, had four wives, two of whom enjoyed the rank of queen. The custom of the dowry was common to both Ireland and Wales in ancient times.

The status of women among the ancient Celts seems therefore to have been quite wretched. Aristotle asserted that domination by women was utterly unknown among the Celts. However, in the mid-1st century AD, in what is now Great Britain, the *Brigantes* were governed by a woman, Cartismandua. Later on, in the year 62 AD, the daughters of the king of the *Iceni*, Prasutagus, laid claim to the kingdom of their father as their own inheritance. In 61

Group making offerings (Museum of Aix-en-Provence).

AD, Boadicea, a woman of royal blood, commanded the army of the ancient Britons. Yet no similar state of affairs can be found among other tribes or at earlier periods. Marriage was certainly a reliable way of forming political alliances; Orgetorix, for example, gave his daughter to Dunmorix, who arranged for his mother to marry a noble Biturige, and also married his sister and female relatives in other politically suitable ways. For these reasons, it is unlikely that women were entirely without influence. As we shall see later on, they were often invoked as arbiters of disputes.

The fidelity of Celtic women was famous throughout the ancient world, as can be seen from certain legends in which they figure. At Sardes, the historian Polybus got to talk to a Galatian woman who was cele-brated for her wisdom and her spiritual qualities. She was Chiomara, the wife of Ortiagon, king of the *Tolistobogii*. She had been taken prisoner in the war with the Romans in 189 BC. A centurion grabbed her and raped her. As it happened, he was both greedy and lustful: he was promised a large sum of money for the ransom of this captive. He led her to the appointed spot. However, no sooner had the Gauls handed over the agreed amount of gold to the centurion, and received Chiomara in return, than she signalled to one of her compatriots to cut the Roman down as she was taking her leave of him. The Gaul obeyed and chopped off the head of the centurion. She picked it up and wrapped it up among the folds of her dress. When she had returned to her husband, she flung the head at his feet. Ortiagon, in utter astonishment, said: "Woman, fidelity is a fine thing".—Yes, she replied, but there is something finer still: and it is that only one man who has been my lover should be allowed to stay alive! In the Irish epics, Derdiu kills herself when the king of Ulster, having spent a year with her, delivers her to her husband's murderer. Like Chiomara, she could not accept the notion that a woman could have two living husbands at the same time.

The heroic devotion of the Gaulish woman Epopine or Empone to her husband Sabinus dates from a period when the Celts had been greatly influenced by Roman civilization.

The misfortunes and the heroism of another Galatian woman, Camma, priestess of Artemis and wife of the tetrarch Sinatos, as related by Plutarch, can be placed in either history or legend, as one wishes, since the evidence is rather uncertain. One of the male relatives of her husband, Sinorix, fell in love with her, and, seeing that he could not prevail over her virtue and her fidelity, killed Sinatos treacherously. He spoke to her of his passion for her, his wealth, and eventually admitted to having killed her husband, out of love for her. At first, Camma recoiled in horror, but then she seemed to accept her new state calmly, and agreed to become his wife. On a prescribed day, in keeping with the ancient rite, she offered him a cup of mead; she poured a few drops onto the ground, drank a little and then invited Sinorix to drink the rest.

The famous remains at Stonehenge (Wiltshire, England).

Left: headless goddess with a child on her knees. Right: terra cotta statuette (both items from the Museum of Saint-Germain-en-Laye).

He drained the goblet to the dregs. Before the arrival of the guests, Camma had mixed a deadly poison with the mead, thus affording herself the satisfaction, while she herself died, of seeing the death of her husband's killer.

Celtic women figure also in historical accounts of the foundation of Marseille, then known as Phocaea. Although it was accepted as authentic by both Aristotle and Trogues Pompeus, the story does seem to be a genealogical fable devised as a way of giving the noble Marseille family of the Protiades a distinguished ancestry. Just as Nannos, king of the *Segobrigii,* was preparing the wedding of his daughter Gyptis (or Petta), two Phocaeans, Simos and Protis (or Euxenos), landed on Celtic soil and asked the king for his friendship and for enough land to found a city. The king invited them to the wedding feast. When all the guests were assembled the young woman came in and her father asked her to offer a goblet to the man whom she chose as her husband. Gyptis turned towards the Greeks and offered the goblet to Protis. Was this a Celtic or a Ligurian custom? It is impossible to say with certainty; while the name *Segobrigii* was certainly Celtic, the area around Marseille in those days was inhabited by Ligurians.

These examples suggest that the ancients were much more indulgent towards Celtic women than their husbands. It was not until the 4th century AD that one comes across accounts of a Celtic custom which implies that the women of Eastern Gaul were frivolous and flirtatious. According to Emperor Julian, the Celts regarded the Rhine as the judge of their wive's fidelity. On the birth of a child, the father would take him and put him on a shield, and then deposit him on the surface of the river. A legitimate child remained afloat while a bastard would sink. One wonders, however, whether these were Celts or Germans. During the time of Julian, *Celtis* was used to denote Germania, as distinct from *Galatia,* Transalpine Gaul.

Besides conjugal fidelity Gaulish women had other qualities. They were big, beautiful, fertile, good nursing mothers and took good care of their children. Our only guide to the occupations of Gaulish women is provided by the obscure text of Strabo, where we learn that the distribution of labor between the sexes was roughly the opposite of what it was among the Greeks, but that this feature was common to many barbarous peoples.

We know for a fact that Celtic women accompanied their menfolk into battle. The wives of the *Helvetii* defended entrenched positions against the Romans; the wives of the Britons encouraged them to greater ardor in combat. Ammianus Marcellinus paints a vivid picture of Gaulish women, coming to the aid of their husbands in the midst of a quarrel; he describes them as being stronger than their husbands, turning green with rage, swinging their enormous white arms, and using

Left: comb depicting a human shape. Opposite: bronze Celtic mirror found in the tomb of a woman at Desborough, England. Below: necklace from the burial ground of Ibiza (Archeological Museum of Madrid).

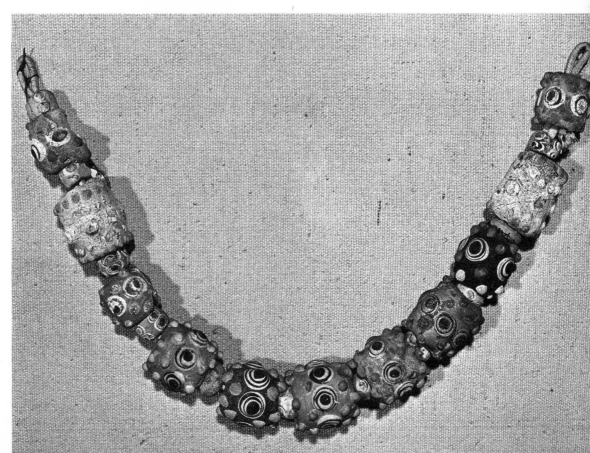

both fists and feet to good effect.

Before the conquest of Cisalpine Gaul by the Gauls they fought a terrible civil war. The women strode forth into the midst of the armies and took the role of arbiters, to resolve the dispute. Plutarch wrote that, from that time forth, the Celts did not hesitate to invite their women to participate in their deliberations on war and peace, and arbitrate any disputes they might have had with their allies. It had been agreed between Hannibal and the Celts that, if the Celts ever had occasion to complain about the Carthaginians, the Carthaginian generals would act as judges, and that, if the Carthaginians had a complaint about the Celts, the dispute would be adjudicated by the Celts' wives.

As for the relations between father and son, Caesar tells us that in Gaul the father had the power of life and death over his children. This was so among the ancient Britons and Irish also. Tadg, the druid of the Irish king Cond, in the 2nd century BC, wanted to have his daughter burnt. King Cairpre had his three sons thrown into the sea as soon as they were born. The Welsh manuscript known as the *Book of Llan Day* contains two similar stories. Caesar reported a most distinctive custom. "The Gauls are unlike the other peoples in that they do not allow their children to address them in public until they have reached the age at which they are capable of performing their military service; they felt it was a disgrace for a man's son to appear in

40

public with him while still a child." This text is difficult to interpret. Can it mean that sons remained with their mothers until they reached the age of military action? Or should one attribute it to the Irish custom of bringing up the children of noble parents away from their own home?

With the exception of the custom, quoted by Aristotle, of plunging new-born children into the cold waters of a river, and also the unusual custom referred to by Julian, the authors of antiquity did not record the Celtic habits pertaining to birth. Death, however, is another matter: here the records are much fuller. The Gauls who took Rome used to bury their dead; and it was not until an epidemic occurred that they began to pile up corpses in order to burn them. The Celtiberians, the Gauls who invaded Greece, used to abandon their dead for the vultures and other scavengers to eat. Plutarch and Pausanias both remarked that the Gauls did not lament the passing of a dead man.

The funerals of the Celts of Gaul, who were relatively highly civilized, were quite splendid, sumptuous affairs. Anything thought to have been valued by the person during his lifetime was put on the pyre along with the body, even domestic animals. According to Caesar, only a short while before his visits to Gaul, they used to burn both the slaves and the preferred clients of the deceased, for the sake of regularity. While the funeral was proceeding, it was customary to toss into the flames letters addressed to dead relatives, as if they could read them. Mela observed that everything which they had found useful during their lifetime was burnt and buried with the deceased.

At the time when bronze was the predominant metal for the manufacture of weapons, incineration was practised in various parts of Gaul, particularly in the southeast and the north. When bronze swords disappeared, to be replaced by iron, burial under artificial mounds (tumuli) or in the earth itself became common. As for the necropolis based on incineration which were characteristic of the period of the Roman conquest in Gaul, they are few in number, and little is known about them. It is quite likely that cremation left few traces, if any, of either the body of the deceased or of the articles which were burnt with him.

In the British Isles and on the continent, incineration seems to have been predominant during the Bronze Age and the Roman conquest. In the Iron Age, bodies were more commonly buried under *tumuli*.

Left: golden horn from Klein-Aspergle. Above: swords from the burial ground of Giubasco (National Museum, Zurich).

Left: top, the largest burial mound in Europe, at Silbury Hill. Below: the burial mound at New Grange, in Ireland, the largest corridor-type dolmen. Above: a covered way at Mougan-en-Commana (Finistère). Below: carved spirals and circles decorating the New Grange burial mound.

Below: Celtic cockerel (Museum of Saint-Germain-en-Laye).

4. THE LAND, HUNTING.
INDUSTRY.

Our knowledge of agriculture, commerce and industry among the Celts dates essentially from the Roman conquest, and the information we have is mainly about Gaul.

Agriculture was the principal activity of the Celts. In this sense, there was a great difference between the Germanic tribes and the Gauls, as the former consumed very little wheat and lived mainly on milk and the flesh of their animals. Cattle was abundant in Gaul, as can be seen from the fact that virtually everyone of Caesar's expeditions led to the seizure of large amounts of livestock. The Germanic tribes used to come to Gaul in the hope of seizing the flocks of the *Eburones*. However, the cultivation of wheat was quite common among the Transalpine Gauls; so much so that Caesar never had difficulty in feeding his armies on any of his campaigns. He got wheat from the *Aedui, Sequani, Lingones, Esubii, Curiosolites, Veneti, Leuci, Remi, Ambiani*. In the vicinity of Avaricum there was an abundance of both wheat and fodder. In order to be prepared for war, the Veneti used to amass reserves of wheat inside their *oppida*. The amount of grain stored at Alesia would have been enough to feed 80,000 persons for a month. Before setting off for Gaul, the Helvetii planted as much grain as they could in order to be sure of having all the wheat they would need for their expedition. When they were driven back into their own country, after they had burnt the wheat they could not carry with

them, they turned to the Allobroges to get what they needed. The varieties of wheat grown in Gaul during the time of Pliny were: *arinca, siligo* (successfully grown only by the Allobroges), and *memini*, a three-month wheat grown in the north.

Besides wheat, which was grown in the fertile fields described for us in the *Commentaries*, we know, from Pliny, that millet *(holcus sorgum)* was grown, most particularly in Aquitaine. Double row barley, known as *galaticum* in the writings of Columelus, is probably of Gaulish origin. In Belgium there were seedless apples called *spadonia*. As for grapes, they were really not grown in Gaul until after the Roman conquest. Winter fodder for cattle consisted largely of turnips. About the time of Pliny flax was being grown quite successfully in Gaul, and the *Cadurci*, the *Ruteni*, the *Bituriges*, the *Caleti* and the *Morini* all produced quite presentable fabrics.

Several names for agrarian units of measurement used by the Romans are of Celtic origin, and are evidence of the importance of questions of measurement among the Gauls. The rural *candetum* was a square of one hundred cubits of one hundred and fifty Roman feet in length. The urban *candetum* measured exactly one hundred Roman feet along each side. The *arepennis* was about 120 feet long and 110 wide. The *leuga*, a unit of length adopted by the Romans, was also a Gaulish measure.

In this way, at the time of the Roman conquest, Gaul was fertile and well cultivated. The Transalpine Gauls were quite as accomplished in the art of farming as their Cisalpine brethren, whose main wealth towards the 3rd century BC, consisted of their livestock and their agrarian skills.

Latin agronomists have left us some information about the agricultural processes of the Gauls. They used a variety of fertilisers, such as white chalk; lime was much in use among the *Aedui* and the *Pictones,* and marl, of which Pliny mentions several kinds, among the Gauls and the Britons. The Cisalpines to the north of the Po used ashes rather than manure on certain soils. The Salassi, at the foot of the Alps, discovered a new technique for fertilisation when sowing their seeds on plowed-over millet.

The idea of adding two small wheels to the plow was first invented in Gaulish Rhetia. On the flat land of the larger landholdings in Gaul, harvesting was done with a sort of two-wheeled cart, the front edge of which was equipped with teeth which removed the ears of grain, tipping them into the cart. A comb was used to pick millet. The Gauls had scythes which could cut taller grass while leaving the short grass untouched. The scythes were sharpened with stones from Transalpine Gaul, known as *passernices.*

The domestic animals bred in Gaul in ancient times were virtually the same as today. The breeds of Cisalpine oxen were re-nowned for their strength and endurance. The cheese obtained from the cows of the Alps and the Cévennes were very famous; cheese was also made from goat's milk. Gaul contained vast flocks of sheep, the value of whose wool varied from one breed to another. Pigs were so large, so fast and so strong that they were a real danger to anyone unfamiliar with them; they provided excellent hams. Geese were taken all the way from Morinia to Rome, the more tired among them being made to walk ahead of the rest.

The armies of Claudius II had brought back to Rome a large number of Celtic mares which were highly prized. The Celts of Gaul went out of their way to find foreign horses and paid a high price for them. In the year 52 there were enough horses in Gaul to mount a cavalry force of some 15,000 men. The mules of Galatia were mentioned by Plutarch. Leather horsecloths were called *Scordisca* in Latin, from the name of the Celtic tribe which had invented them, the *Scordisci.*

Celtic dogs, particularly those of the Morines, the Britons and the Belgians, were highly reputed. Those known as *vertragi* were very fast runners. According to Pliny, the Gauls used to mate their bitches with wolves, the offspring from such unions then serving as leader of the pack. The continental Celts used Breton dogs in battle. The Arvernian king Bituitos had a guard made up of dogs, and was quite confident that they would dispose of the Ro-

man army in a few mouthfuls. In Irish epic legend, a dog known as Ailbe stood guard, all alone, over the entire kingdom of Laighen.

After war, hunting was the main occupation of the Celts. They were certainly accomplished at it. Those who hunted for pleasure, rather than in earnest, used no nets. The richer Celts would send men out at dawn to reconnoitre for the presence of a hare at rest; as soon as one was sighted, they went to the place indicated, and, after rousing their quarry, they would send their dogs after it. Two sorts of dog were used: one sort tracked down the animal by following its scent, while the others stood at the point where it was thought likely the hare would emerge from cover, so as to leap on him for the kill. Whenever they killed an animal, the Celts would set aside a small amount of money—two obols for a hare, a drachma for a fox and four drachmas for a deer. At the end of the year, during the celebrations of the birthday of Artemis, the treasure thus formed was opened and used to pay for a sacrifice to the goddess and a banquet at which the dogs appeared bedecked with flowers.

When hunting birds, the Celts used a hand-thrown dart. Arrows intended for use in hunting were poisoned with the juice of the fruit of a tree not unlike the fig-tree, the fruit of which looked something like the capital of a Corinthian column. According to Pliny, this poison was derived from the white hellebore.

48

Left: figurine and assorted ornaments (Marne).
Above: dog depicted on vase.

Fishing clearly did not occupy nearly the same place as hunting in the Celtic range of pleasures. Certain Breton tribes, as we have seen, took no advantage of the abundance of fish available off their shores. Pliny claimed that the inhabitants of the Mediterranean coast used trained dolphins when they were fishing; they let their helpmates have a part of the catch, and, in addition, gave them some bread soaked in wine.

In the Celtic world, silver mines were located pincipally in the Pyrenees, and the regions occupied by the *Gabali* and the *Ruteni*. There were also many silver mines in Spain. Gaul contained many iron ore mines, and the Gauls were expert at working them. There were few of them in the British Isles, however. The Britons used copper for their coins, and also iron rings of a given weight. The *Caledonii* wore iron ornaments around their neck and on their bellies, this being regarded as a sign of great wealth. Copper was to be found in Aquitaine and in the territory of the *Ceutrones*, but the Gauls did not know how to process it properly. In the British Isles, imported copper was used. Lead was found

49

commonly throughout Gaul and the British Isles.

Tin occurred only in the British Isles. It was mined near what was then known as Cape Belerion, and carted at low tide across to the Isle of Wight (then known as *Ictis*), where merchants would come to buy it.

The Gauls used coral and enamel for decorative purposes. The finest coral was collected off the southern coast of Gaul. It was used for the ornamentation of swords, shields and helmets. In fact, the use of coral in the ancient world was restricted more or less completely to those areas which had been under Celtic influence, or to the Celtic regions themselves. Coral is found particularly often in Gaul, particularly in the territory of the *Remi,* in burial grounds, together with amber pearls, glass beads, gold jewelry, etc., but never with coins. The principal use to which coral was put was the decoration of bronze items, clasps, buttons, harnesses, scabbards, helmets, bracelets, chains, pinheads; on necklaces it was often used as a pendant. According to Pliny, coral was thought to have certain curative properties; a branch of coral around the neck of a child, for example, was regarded as protection against harm. Objects decorated with coral most probably belong to the end of the Hallstatt period and the first part of the Tène period.

Philostratus wrote that the barbarians from the oceanic coasts knew how to pour white, black, yellow and red colors on incandescent copper so that they hardened permanently to the consistence of stone, keeping the designs made on the metal. He must have been referring to the Celts and an enamelling process. This art was certainly practised among the *Aedui.* Enamel has been recovered in various forms among the ruins of *Bibractium:* ingots, scrap and wire-edging; indeed, a whole district of the city seems to have been devoted to the enamelling business. Enamel was applied to objects such as buttons, clasps and broaches.

Above: detail from a bas-relief of a plow (the "Merchants' Dolmen" at Locmariaquer). Right: plow at the Luxembourg State Museum (Tène civilisation).

Decorated stone from Tre-castle, Wales. Right: fragment of bas-relief depicting a woodcutter.

5. DIVINITIES. DIVINATION. FORMS OF WORSHIP.

Caesar's writings provide us with our fullest source of information on the Gaulish gods. He, in turn, seems to be expressing not so much his own personal observations, but those of earlier writers. The god most honored by the Gauls was Mercury, in his opinion; he was regarded by them as the inventor of all the arts, as the guide of travellers, and the sponsor of all profitable business dealings and trade. Next came Apollo, Mars, Jupiter and Minerva. The Gaulish conception of these gods was more or less the same as that of other nations: Apollo cures sickness, Minerva teaches the elements of industry and the arts, Jupiter holds a sway over the empire of the skies, Mars is supreme in war. Once they decided to go to war, they invoked the assistance of Mars and vowed to dedicate the spoils of war to him.

This part of Caesar's writings has come in for some criticism. Is it possible for all the Gaulish tribes, which, by Caesar's own admission, differed in language, customs and laws, to have had the same five divinities? What were the names of these gods and this goddess in their own Celtic tongue? Is such an assimilation between these five divinities and five Roman divinities at all plausible?

At the time of the Celtic migrations their main god resembles Ares-Mars. Among the *Insubres* there was a temple of Athena in which the emblems of war have been found. In 223, the Celts vowed to dedicate Roman arms to Vulcan. For this reason,

Left: bas-relief of the god Mars (Chalon-sur-Saône).
Right: triumphant warrior.

57

one should add to the Celtic pantheon, as reconstituted by Caesar, a sixth god which could be assimilated to the Roman god Vulcan.

The Celts living on the Atlantic coast had a particular veneration for the Dioscures, who, according to an ancient Celtic tradition, originally arrived by sea.

It is interesting to note that the noun used among the Indo-European peoples to designate the notion of divinity, *dewos,* exists in all the Celtic languages: Irish *dia,* Welsh *dwy* and Breton *doué.* The root of this word, *div, deiv,* means "shine". *Deivos* must therefore be the light of day deified. At what period was this god replaced among the Celts by the god of night?

Dion Cassius referred to a goddess of victory, Andate of Andraste, among the Bretons of Boudicca and claimed that human sacrifices were offered to her. The name of this goddess seems to be a corruption of the Greek word for *The Inevitable.* Be that as it may, there was a goddess of the *Voconces* who was actually called Andarta; moreover, most of the altars of Victory discovered in the south of Gaul occurred in the region occupied in ancient times by the *Voconces.*

In Gaulish inscriptions it is possible to find the names of certain Celtic divinities: *Brigindo* (cf. *Brigantia*); *Anvalonnacos* (cf. the god *Anvalo*); and *Alisanos,* which is also found in a Latin inscription, *Deo Alisanu.*

The most interesting inscriptions are those attached to some figurative monument or other. The most curious of these are the two altars found in Paris in 1710, and now in the museum at Cluny. One face of the first altar shows a lumberjack chopping down a tree; it bears the name of Esus. Another face is adorned with a bull carrying three birds somewhat like cranes, two on its back and one on its head; the background of the bas-relief consists of foliage; the inscription bears the words *tarvos trigaranus,* which can be easily explained through the Irish word *tarbh,* Breton *tarv* ("bull"), the Irish and the Breton *tri* ("three"), and the Breton and Welsh *garan* ("crane"). It thus means the "bull with three cranes". On the two other faces are images of Jupiter *(iovis)* and Volcanus, two gods with human heads adorned with ram's horns. The name carved above the sculpture is *Cernunnos.* On another face is a bearded man armed with a club with which he is threatening a snake. The Gaulish word *Smer (tull)os* can be discerned here. On the other faces are Castor, and Pollux, with their horses.

The various figures on this monument have often been compared with similar figures elsewhere. The altar at Reims has a seated god, with crossed legs; with his right hand he is squeezing a bag from which grains are falling and being eaten by a stag and a bull in the lower half of the bas-relief. On his head this god has stag's antlers; on his right is an Apollo, and on his left a

Mercury. The altar at Vandeuvres (Indre) has a god with stag's antlers, in a Buddhic pose; he is pressing a wineskin between his hands; on his left and right are two figures standing on dragons; one of them is holding a necklace in his hands. On one of the sides of the altar there is an Apollo holding a lyre. This half-human and half-animal god occurs also with the god with the wheel and the boar on the Gundestrup cauldron. He is comparable to the dragon with the head of a ram adorning the three-headed altars, the side of a niche containing a figure of Hermes, and the Gundestrup cauldron. It is possible that, in the mythical history of Ireland, the Fomore, antagonists of the *Tuatha de Danaan* and a warlike people whose epithet was *goborchind* ("goat's head") may have been related to the divinity we have just described.

The Trèves altar depicts a lumberjack chopping down a tree. On the branches of the tree are three cranes, with a bull's head visible in the surrounding foliage. This must have been an abridged reproduction of the myth represented on two faces of the Paris altar. S. Reinach, having compared the two altars, showed that Tarvos Trigaranus and Esus belong to the same scene. This scene, however, is quite difficult to interpret.

The sculpted menhir at Kernuz (Finistère) has sculpted figures over 4 ft. tall on each of its four faces. They are thought to represent Mercury, Hercules, Mars and, jointly, Sucellos and Nantosuelta.

The Roman goddess Epona, who is often represented in the form of a woman sitting on a horse, is almost certainly of Celtic origin; her name can be traced to the Celtic *ebeul*, "foal" (compare the Gaulish word *apo-redias*, horse driver). It has proved possible to reconstruct a group consisting of a seated goddess holding a patera and fruits, a female bear and a tree, all standing on a pedestal bearing the words: *Deae Artioni* (*arth* is the Welsh for bear). A bas-relief found near Haguenau shows a figure holding in its left hand a spear, while leaning with its right hand on a bull's head. One wonders whether this might not be a god whose name is cognate with the name *Mider*, the hero of Irish legend.

Some images have survived of the water gods: a fragment of a statue of the goddess *Sequana*, and a bust of divinity named *Dirona*. The Rhine, from which Virdomarus claimed to have been born might well have been so named by the Celts, who may also have inaugurated or continued the cult of the river, though it is difficult to be definitive about this question. The Irish *rian* = *reno* means "sea". The reader will recall that the Celts used to appoint the river Rhine as arbiter in disputes concerning their wive's fidelity.

Should the names of the mountain divinities—names such as *Vosegus*, god of the Vosges, Arduinna, goddess of the forest of the Ardennes and Abnoba, goddess of the Black Forest—also be regarded as Celtic?

There are two inscriptions which are evidence of the worship accorded to a deified city: Bibractium, the metropolis of the Eduens. The *dea Aventia* was without a doubt the protectress of Aventicum. According to one author the name of Lyon, *Lugudunum*—the second part of which is the well known Celtic name *dunos,* in Irish *dun,* "fortress"—begins with the name of a Gaulish god, Lugus. It is, to say the least, curious that the feast of Augustus was celebrated in Lyon on the 1st of August, while that same date, in Old Irish, is known as *Lug-nasad,* or festival of Lug. It is claimed that the date chosen for the emperor's festival was precisely the date of the ancient festival in honor of the god of the town itself.

The Celts were more accomplished at telling the future from omens than most of the other peoples of antiquity. Dejotarus was renowned as a remarkable sooth-sayer. Birds such as crow and the eagle were closely involved in divination; the Bretons even used the hare as a means of telling the future. Birds were thought to show armies the direction they should take; Dejotarus, alerted by an eagle, once changed course in battle. According to Artemidoris (1st century BC), in a harbor somewhere on the Atlantic coast, there were two crows each with one light-colored wing. People involved in a dispute used to place a number of pastries on a piece of wood, arranging them so that they could not be confused with those of the other parties. The crows would then fly down onto the pastries, eating some and scattering the rest; that party which had had its cakes scattered by the crows won the dispute.

In ancient times certain animals were worshipped; among the Bretons, the goose, the hen and the hare were all taboo. The Galatians of Pessinunte ate no pork. The god Mercury's second name was Moccus, which means pig. As is well known, the wild boar was the battle emblem of the Celts, and it is in this capacity that it appears on the triumphal arch at Orange. According to Tacitus, the *Aestii,* who looked and behaved like the *Suevi,* though they spoke a language closely related to Breton, used to wear miniature symbols of the wild boar as a talisman. Nennius wrote about a marvellous animal, *porcus troit,* which was pursued by King Arthur in a fantastic hunting episode; this was the *twrch trwyth* of the Welsh story entitled *Kulhwch and Olwen.* It seems clear that this famous boar in Celtic legend must have been a memory of the ancient times when the pig had been the symbol and the totem of a Gaulish tribe. On Gaulish coins the emblems found more often than any other are those of the horse and the boar. The pediment of an altar at Reims has a picture of a rat, while the small three-headed altar found in the same city is crowned by the head of a ram. A bird appears on the lower part of the altar at Sarrebourg. We have already spoken of the bull with the three cranes, the snake with

Hunting scene (Clonmacnois).

the head of a ram, and the gods with the heads of a stag and a ram—all of which are only marginally reminiscent of the ancient worship of sacred animals by the Celts.

Like the Romans, the Celts sought to determine the future by examining the entrails of sacrificial victims; they also attached much weight to the evidence of dreams. Certain physical phenomena used to fill them with fear. In 218, the Galatians who were allied with Attala, were so frightened by an eclipse of the moon that they refused to go any further.

However, we have found no monument providing evidence of the worship of trees, unless, that is, one is to include the two faces of the Paris altar and the altar at Trèves, on which trees and foliage are to be seen. Yet we do know, through Pliny, that the robur oak was, for the Gauls, the tree of the sacred forests, and that they performed no ceremony without using its foliage. Maximus of Tyr writes that a tall oak tree was the Celtic representation of Zeus. We also learn in a passage in the writings of Pliny that the *Lycopodium selago* was thought to help prevent accidants, and that mistletoe, which was called by a name meaning "universal remedy", was a remedy against poisons and infertility, even among animals. Since mistletoe rarely occurs on the robur oak, it was regarded as a sign from heaven.

The picking of mistletoe, Pliny tells us, was done on the sixth day after the full moon. After sacrifices and meals had been

The god Esus picking mistletoe. Right: painting
from the early 20th century of a druidic scene.

prepared in keeping with the rites, under the tree, two white bulls were brought along, their horns tied together. A priest, dressed in white, climbed the tree and cut the mistletoe with a golden sickle, passing it down to his acolytes below, who received it on a white sash. The victims were then sacrificed, and the god was asked to make this gift to him propitious to those who were offering it.

These miraculous plants also included *Samolus Valerandi,* a remedy against foot-and-mouth disease. Special procedures had to be followed: the person picking the plant had to be fasting, had to use his left hand, was not allowed to look at it, and was obliged to put it solely in the trough in which it was to be crushed. Verbena was used by the Gauls for the drawing of lots and for divination. Prophecy by means of marked pieces of wood, which Tacitus attributes to the Germanic tribes, was known among the Gaelic tribes and the Bretons.

In the time of Pliny, the sacred woods of the Celts were made up principally of robur oaks, as can be seen from various ancient authors. The Galatians of Asia Minor had a senate which met to judge murder cases in a place the name of which, in Celtic, meant "sacred wood". There is some reason to believe that these sacred woods served as temples, because Caesar constantly talks of the consecrated place, *in loco consecrato,* on the territory of the Carnutes, where the druids used to gather

each year at a set time in order to administer justice.

Within the temples and the sacred enclosures, the Celts used to amass vast quantities of gold which they offered to the gods; and, although all Celts loved money, none of them dared to touch it. The *Arvernes* had hung up in one of their temples the sword which Caesar had left in their hands; yet the conqueror of Gaul, when he saw it there some time later, refused to lay a hand on it, since he felt that he could not touch a sacred object.

The Celtic forms of worship involved prayers and probably dancing, libations and sacrifices. The Breton queen Boadicea invoked Adraste by raising a hand towards the sky. The druids from the isle of Mona used to pray by raising their hands above their heads and hurling the most frightful oaths and incantations against the enemy. According to Eudoxius, the eastern Galatians had special rites which they performed whenever they were invaded by a plague of grasshoppers, and which actually had the desired effect of summoning the assistance of the birds. When engaged in worship, the Gauls turned to the right; the Irish of the Middle Ages also thought that turning to the right brought good luck. One wonders whether Vercingetorix might not have been obeying the same impulse when he turned around Caesar on his horse. As related by Artemidoris, the religious ceremonies in use on one of the off-shore islands of Britain were strongly

67

reminiscent of the cult of Demeter and Core on the island of Samothrace.

It was through dance, by the light of the full moon, that the Celtiberians celebrated the ritual worship of a god whose name has been lost. The Boians of Cisalpine Gaul used the skull of proconsul Postumius, adorned with gold, as a sacred vase for offering libations during religious festivals.

Sacrifices were more often than not human. In the year 75 BC, Cicero wrote of the atrocious custom of human sacrifice among the barbarian Gauls. According to Caesar, the Gauls thought that the life of a man was the only way of redeeming that of another man, and that the immortal gods could not be placated in any other way. Among certain tribes, this sort of sacrifice was a part of State policy. Some tribes used to erect huge effigies *(simulacra)* with limbs of woven osier, which they filled with live men; then they would light the fire and watch their fellows perish. They felt that the agony of those who had been found guilty of theft, highway robbery or some other crime was the kind of sacrifice which the gods liked best. However, when such victims were in short supply they made up their numbers with innocent men.

According to Strabo the victim was stabbed in the back with a saber; the future was then forecast on the basis of his convulsions; sometimes the victim was shot to death with arrows, crucified in the temples, or burnt alive inside a huge wooden effigy, which also contained cattle and other an-imals. Diodorus of Sicily wrote that the Gauls used to keep their criminals in prison for five years, and then, in honor of the gods, they impaled them and burnt them with numerous other offerings on large pyres. Human sacrifice, particularly during war, is referred to by writers both before and after Caesar.

Dion Cassius reported that the Britons of Boadicea used to slaughter captive women with all manner of refinement, in honor of the goddess Adraste, while we learn from Justinian that the Gallo-Greeks used to offer sacrifices before going into battle; one day, when the omens were particularly bad, they even slaughtered their own wives and children in order to appease the wrath of the gods. Tacitus describes the horrible superstition of the inhabitants of Mona, who sprinkled their altars with human blood as part of their religious rituals, and who consulted the gods by scrutinizing the entrails of their victims.

In the year 97 BC a senate decree was issued prohibiting human sacrifice. Denys of Halicarnasse, who finished his *Roman Antiquities* about 8 BC, noted that human sacrifices were still customary in the Gaul of his day. In 77, it seems that human sacrifice was still common practice in those parts of the British Isles which had remained independent; however, in Gaul, about the year 40 AD, the druids merely let some blood from men under a special oath, without putting them to death. The ancient barbarities were nothing more than

a distant memory. In Ireland, the *Dinn-Senchus,* a geographical treatise which, in parts dates back to the 11th century BC, mentioned an idol named Cromm Cruach in whose honor children were still being immolated in the early years of the Christian era.

Among the religious beliefs of the Celts, the one which most astonished the rest of the ancient world was belief in the immortality of the soul. Valerius Maximus wrote: "I would call the Celts utterly stupid were it not for the fact that the opinion of these men in breeches is simply that of Pythagoras clad in pallium." Other writers thought that this doctrine had reached the Celts via the druids. In any case, it was very widespread and popular. This accounts for the Celtic custom of lending people money

to be repaid in the next world, agreeing that hell should be the site for the settlement of their business disputes and burning, with the dead, all the objects which the living still used in their everyday lives. According to Pomponius Mela, people were sometimes seen leaping into the flames which were consuming their relatives' dead bodies, so as to be near them in the world to come.

The Celts claimed to have no fear of earthquakes or floods; indeed, more than once they were seen advancing, fully armed, into the waves. Their faith in a future life was certainly the kind of attitude which exalts one's courage, and was probably also the cause of the religious suicides which were observed among them. It might also perhaps account for the human sacri-

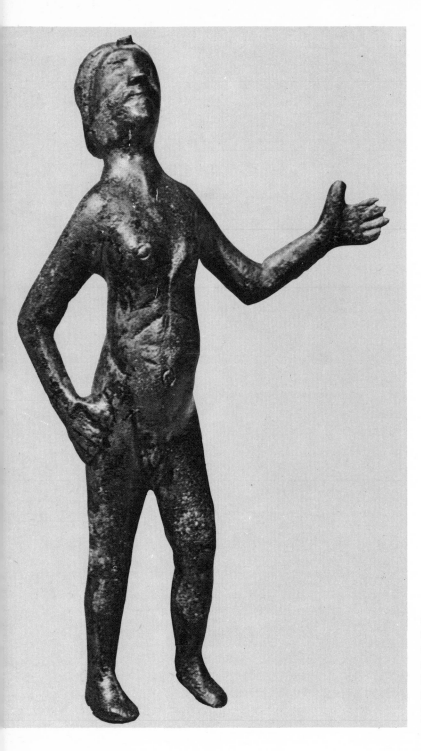

Bronze figures of dancers, from the Gallo-Roman period (Museum of Orleans). Following pages: ornaments from the head of a spit (bronze, Basse-Yutz, Moselle, France). Celtic cross at Wadebridge.

fices which we have just referred to. The idea of replacing burial by cremation might also have something to do with their notion of the survival of souls after death.

Although texts on this point are obscure and contradictory, it seems unlikely that this immortality consisted in a second life on earth in a new body. Rather, it was felt that the same breath would sustain men's souls in another world, death being simply the middle point in a long journey. The position of this other world varies depending on the geographical location of the various Celtic tribes. Anatole Le Braz has pointed out that the peoples living on the mainland of Europe tended to place the other world on an island. A tradition which Procopius recorded in writing in the 6th century had the inhabitants of the regions situated immediately opposite the British Isles being responsible for taking the souls of the dead across the Channel to the island beyond. In the middle of the night, they would hear someone knocking on their door and a voice whispering to them. Then, they would go down to the beach, driven by some mysterious force; there they would find boats which while apparently empty were so heavily loaded down with the souls of the dead that they were riding very low in the water. In less than an hour they reached their destination, whereas the trip would normally take a whole day. On arrival in the isle of the Bretons, they would see no-one, but hear a voice calling out the names of their pas-

Menhir facing the sea, on the Quiberon peninsula (Morbihan).

75

sengers one by one.

Plutarch wrote of an equally strange tradition. On an island near Brittany, there lived men whom the Bretons regarded as sacred and inviolable. No sooner had Demetrius landed there than a great wind started blowing, with flashes of flame tearing the sky. The inhabitants of the island told him that a great man had just passed away. According to Plutarch, the island of Saturn, where men were thought to converse with the spirits, was situated five days' sailing time away from the British Isles.

The epic literature of Ireland is the only source from which we can form an idea of the Elyseum which the Gaelic peoples longed for—a land of wonders, which could be reached after a journey in a boat made of glass. Beyond the seas there was a great transparent tower with a rather blurred outline; shapes similar to those of men could be seen on the battlements. Anyone trying to land at the foot of the tower was carried away by the surging waves. Beyond the tower, fertile plains, covered with strange trees, stretched away into the distance. Some of these trees had silver branches with golden apples on them. When these apples touched each other, they emitted a beautiful sound which instantly made everyone within earshot forget all their woes. Streams of wine and mead flowed at the foot of the trees, while the rain descending from the heavens soaked the earth with beer. The swine

grazing in the meadows would come to life again as soon as they had been slaughtered, so as to provide meat for yet another round of banquets. Wherever one went, gentle music delighted the ear with its graceful melodies.

Left: Stone of Destiny, at Tara, Ireland. The ancient kings of Ireland were crowned on this stone. Above: view of the site of Tara.

Human figure, statue from Boa Island.

6. BARDS AND DRUIDS.

According to Strabo each of the Celtic peoples granted special honors to three categories of men: the bards, the *vates* and the druids. Diodorus tells us that the Gauls had poets known as bards, and that they also had theologians, who enjoyed great esteem, known as druids, and also divines who were deeply venerated. Ammianus Marcellinus considered that the Gauls had been civilized by the bards, the *euhages* and the druids. Caesar mentions only the druids, though it seems likely that he understood this term in a general sense, covering the druids properly so called, the divines and perhaps also the bards. The term *druid* could therefore be said to apply to all men following what, in those days, constituted the liberal professions.

In ancient Ireland there were three sorts of lettered man: the bards, *bard*; the druids, *drui, druad*; and the *file*. Quite early on, the bards were replaced as panegyric or satirical poets, by the *file*, who at the same time performed the functions of divines and judges, and who were divided into several classes, depending the number of epic stories they could relate from memory. In Wales, the bard was the eighth of the officials of the royal court.

When entoning their songs of praise or reproach, the bards accompanied themselves on instruments like lyres. In the third book of his *Histories*, Poseidonios tells us that the Celts, when going off to war, used to take with them companions known as table-companions who proclaimed the merits of their masters to all kinds of gatherings, and also, in private, to anyone who might happen to be listening. These men were poets, who sang their subject's praise. They also sang accounts of the illustrious deeds of the great, and kept alive, through their poems, the memory of the fallen heroes of the past.

Like their counterparts in Wales and Ireland, the Gaulish bards composed satirical verse, as well as panegyrics.

The Gaulish bards depicted by Poseidonios and Appian were supported by the patronage of the rich. A rich Arvernian named Luernios once gave a banquet to which his poet came late. He at once began to sing verses in praise of the king and by way of apology for his late arrival. Luernios was so delighted by his performance that he sent for a small bag of gold and tossed it to the bard who was constantly at his side. Having picked it up, the poet sang again, this time saying that the marks left on the ground by the royal carriage wheels brought happiness and wealth to men. The legend of Bituitos, son of Luernios and king of the Arvernians also involves a bard. This was about the time when Cn. Domitius, in the year 122 BC, led an expedition against the Allobroges from the territory of the *Salyi*, a Gaulish people which had settled around Aix and Arles. An envoy from Bituitos came to meet him. He was followed by a poet, who, in the barbaric style, sang the praises of king Bituitos, then the Allobroges, then the envoy himself, exalting their birth and courage and power. Appian goes on to add, tongue in cheek, that illustrious envoys habitually brought such people with them for precisely this sort of reason.

The bards' lyre was doubtless the instrument which Fortunatus called *chrotta* and which he attributed to the Bretons; the name of the *chrotta* was closely related to that of the harp used by the ancient Irish bards, *cruith,* and the Breton bards, *crwth.*

It would appear that the name *bard* was in use in various part of the Celtic world. In northern Italy, for example, there is a village near Milan called *Bardomagus* ("field of the bard"). A Helvetian was called Bardus, and the same name is to be found in Carinthia, Vienna, Styria and Misena (Italy).

The name *bard* was also used in Germany, where the word *barditus,* according to Tacitus, meant the kind of chant commonly sung before a battle, so as to inflame the military ardor of the Germanic tribes.

The earliest mention of the name *druid* occurs in Diogenes Laertius' *Life of the Philosophers,* in which he claims that philosophy started among the barbarians, that the first philosophers were the Persian Magi at Babylon, the Chaldaeans in Assyria, the Gymnosophites in India and the druids among the Celts and the Galatians.

The name *druid* is not satisfactorily explained by the Celtic languages. The Greek etymology of this word, whereby the druids were the "men of the oaks", has proved attractive to many scholars, starting with Pliny the Elder. Were it not for the appearance of the word *drui* in the earliest texts of Irish literature, one might have sought an explanation in the form of a translation or of a popular Greek etymology of some unknown Celtic words.

The institution of the druids did not exist among the Celts of Italy, of the Celtiberians of Spain, the Galatians of Thrace and Asia Minor nor the Celts of the Danube. We cannot be certain, moreover, that it had extended throughout Gaul at any time. It is thought that it first came into being in the British Isles and spread thence to Gaul. Gauls wishing to become more fully acquainted with it used to cross the Channel to Britain. We have no information from early times on druidism in the British Isles. Irish druidism is our only point of reference when considering what the writers of antiquity have to say about the druids of Gaul.

The religious functions of the druids mainly involved attendance at the ceremonies, while they were also responsible for the conduct of sacrifices, both public and private. It appears, curiously enough, that their presence during the ceremonies was more in response to the wishes of the people, and that they did not actually play a principal role in the sacrifice itself. Strabo and Diodorus agree on this point. According to Strabo the Celts made their sacrifices

Stone with ribbed markings and Irish names.

with the assistance of the druids, while Diodorus wrote that, in keeping with their customs, the Celts never offered a sacrifice without a philosopher present, feeling that such men, as they were able to speak the language of the gods and understood them more fully, would greatly help their sacrifices, whether offered in thanks or as a plea for divine favors, to achieve their objective.

Fortune telling was one of the arts practised by the druids. Diviciacus used to announce the feature both by observation of the birds and by conjecture. In the opinion of Caesar, the druids interpreted the will of the gods: *religiones interpretantur.* During the time of Tacitus the Gaulish druids declared that the burning down of the Capitol foreshadowed the imminent fall of the Roman Empire.

At the time of Pliny magic was very popular in Gaul and the British Isles, and the druids, whose name he translated as *magi,* were, in his opinion, magicians and fetishists who held all kinds of magical secrets and medical remedies. The Gaulish druids were the ones who claimed that *lycopodium selago* prevented accidents and that smoke was good for all diseases of the eyes. They also thought the mistletoe of the robur oak had special sacred powers. They also described the method to be used if one wished to seize a serpent's egg: it should be thrown up in the air, and caught on a *sagum* before it landed on the ground, after which one should flee on horseback, because serpents usually chase their quarry until they come across a stream or river. All these things had to be done at a certain quarter of the moon. This egg was sure to bring success in legal disputes and would open the doors of kings. Pliny, however, relates how a noble of the territory of the Voconces was inexplicably put to death by Emperor Claudius, though he had such an egg under his tunic at the time.

While sacrifices and divination were two important religious practices in ancient times, magic secrets, which in the time of Pliny were entrusted to druids, were normally left for sorcerers of lesser repute. How can we reconcile the notion that the druids were both physical and moral philosophers with the rather humble role which Pliny the Naturalist ascribes to them? The difference of dates might help provide an explanation. Caesar and Pliny were separated in time by the reign of Tiberius, who suppressed the druids, and the reign of Claudius who completely abolished the frightfully cruel druidic religion which, in the time of Augustus, had been forbidden to everyone except Roman citizens. Under Pomponius Mela the druids used to teach in restricted places, such as caves or hidden forest clearings. Persecution was not conducive to the maintenance of the lofty moral traditions which had made of the druids the highest-ranking persons in Gaul and the most just of men. Another possibility is that, from the earliest times, the druids had always sought to consolidate their power not merely by their knowledge, but also by the practice of certain magical arts which they themselves were the first to discount as absurd; then, when Roman domination caused them to lose their judicial and political roles, all that was left for them was the pathetic exercise of crude quackery.

The Irish druids are seen mainly as magicians and prophets, foretelling the future, interpreting the secret will of the fairies and casting lots. Through formulas and incantations they were thought to be able to find hidden persons, bring down all sorts of ills on an enemy, cause a thick fog to rise between two armies, make the snow fall, change day to night and make barren women pregnant. They had mastered the secret of potions which could make one forget everything. They had the power to impose obligations, *geis,* which no-one could evade, and to make certain objects taboo. These *geis* were of various sorts: a warrior might be forbidden to tell his name to an enemy; Mael Dunn was not allowed to take with him three companions more than a certain number determined by a druid, while Noïse was not allowed to come to Ireland in peace-time except with three men—Cuchulainn, Conall and Fergus. Fergus had been ordered, in this way, never to refuse an invitation and never to leave a banquet before it was over. Cuchulainn was obliged to stop and accept food from any household he passed, while he was not allowed to eat dog.

Figure of a bull on stone in Morayshire, Scotland.

During the Feast of the Bull a white bull was put to death; a man then ate as much of the bull's meat, and drank as much of the broth as he could; then the man went to sleep and four druids entoned a chant of justice over his sleeping body. In his sleep, the man was supposed to see a vision of the man who was to be king, his face, his deeds and his reputation. On waking up, this man related his dream to the kings. The predictions of the druids dealt with the birth, glory and future misfortunes of a child, the lethal effect of a weapon, and an act of vengeance threatened by a defeated warrior against his conqueror.

Sacrifices were not common in Ireland; it appears even than all references to offerings to the gods were deleted from the Irish texts; however, in scholarly glosses on these texts one does come across the Gaelic word for *victim* and *sacrifice*. In a *Latin life of Saint Patrick* we learn that, at the *Fes Temrach*, or Festival of Tara, the princes of the kingdom, the nobles and the chiefs of the provinces, together with the master of the druids, *druidum magistri*, used to assemble in order to offer victims to the idols. At the funeral of a chief, his animals were slaughtered over his grave; this was a custom among the Gauls in the time of Caesar.

What, however, is the relationship between the colorful accounts to be found in popular tradition and the religion actually professed by the ancient Celts? The Irish druids moved in a world of fairylike wonder, where the most incredible stories could gain credence, and, at the same time, in a

distinctly unsophisticated society in which practices resembling witchcraft seem to have had the status of religious belief. Fetishism is virtually absent, doubtless because the Christian narrators who told posterity of the Irish epics chose to delete anything idolatrous as they went along.

The druids thought that the subject of their teaching should not be put down in writing. The main tenet of their doctrine was that the soul does not perish after death, as it merely passes into the body of someone else. Their doctrine and their teachings also embodied a vast number of questions about the stars and their movements, the size of the earth, the law of nature and the power and influence of the immortal gods. Besides natural physiology or philosophy they also concerned themselves with ethics or moral philosophy. While affirming the immortality of both souls and the world, the druids also taught that, one day, fire and water would come to prevail; Poseidonios, who, like other doxographers, did his best to find Greek influence among the most diverse peoples, attributed this theory to the Gaulish druids though he may have been misled in this case by certain superficial analogies.

Pomponius Mela, confirming the findings of the druids, claimed that their teaching was secret, and that the only feature of it which was public knowledge was the eternity of souls and the existence of another life after death. Diogenes Laertius has preserved for us, in Greek, a maxim which he attributed to the druids: "honor the gods, do no evil, be brave". There are no grounds for supposing that druidic science and philosophy were in any way comparable to the science and philosophy of the Greeks.

We cannot tell whether the druids, like the Roman pontiffs, were responsible for preparing the calender. The Celtic year can be discerned only through Irish and Welsh texts.

Like the other Indo-European peoples, the Celts had a lunar year. The word for month is often confused with that for the moon itself. In Sanskrit, *mas* means "moon" and "month"; the Gothic *mena* means "moon". Old High German *mano* means "moon" and "month". The months and years both began with the full moon.

The Celts were accustomed to counting in nights, as Caesar confirmed in his descriptions of the Celtic world. In ancient Irish and Welsh literature, dates are often reckoned on the basis of nights: the Welsh word for week is *wythnos,* or "eight nights", while a fortnight is *pythefnos,* "fifteen nights"; in Irish *oidhche Samhain* "night of Samhain" (1. November) designated the night preceding, and not following the 1st November.

Nothing precise is known about the duration of the Celtic year.

We do know that it was divided into two halves, since this division is often mentioned in Irish and Welsh texts. But the most common division was into four quarters; it is referred to in both Irish and Welsh law.

The subdivisions of the month are indicated by the Welsh word *pythefnos* and the Irish *coicthiges;* the Welsh *wythnos* which we dealt with above is a division, in round figures, of the fortnight. The period of three days and three nights which is often found in Welsh and Irish texts of antiquity is doubtless an old subdivision of the lunar month lasting 29$\frac{1}{2}$ days.

Druidic teaching, which was long in favor in Gaul during its independence, did not survive for long after the conquest. In Ireland, the druids were surrounded by numerous disciples. Cathbad had a hundred men under him learning the druidic arts, *druidecht.* In one of the legends associated with the life of Saint Patrick, two druids were entrusted with the education of the two daughters of the king Loegaire.

What precisely did druidic teaching involve? A gloss of the *Senchus Mor,* a compilation of Irish jurisprudence, tells us that the Irish druids claimed to have actually made the heavens, the land, the sea, sun, moon, etc. This might well have been the last utterance of that druidic cosmogony in which so many scholars have been inclined to detect great scientific profundity. Moreover, these druids taught magic; the only writings attributed to them in legend consist of ogham characters engraved on four willow wands which were used for divination purposes. As for the doctrine of the immortality of the soul, which was gener-

ally recognized in Ireland before the advent of Christianity, it does not seem to have been specially taught.

The druids were thought to be the most just among men. For this reason they were made judges in public and private disputes. If a crime had been committed, if a murder had taken place, or if there was some dispute about inheritances or limits, they were the ones who decided and who set the amount of fines and the type of punishment to be inflicted. If anyone, whether private individual or public official, rejected their rulings, they were empowered to deny him the right to participate in sacrifices. This was indeed the most severe punishment of all, as the person involved became ostracized, and all contact with him was thought to lead to calamity for those who sought it; if such a person were to lodge a complaint, they would be denied access to the processes of justice, and could hold no public office of any sort. At a set point in the year the druids met on the territory of the Carnutes, at a sacred place. All those involved in litigation used to assemble with them at this place, and carry out their judgments.

One of the subjects which has most intrigued those historians who, lacking precise information, have tried to reconstruct druidism from the resources of their imaginations, is that of the druidesses. Velleda, who gave her name to one of the most dramatic characters of Chateaubriand's *Martyrs,* was a prophetess from Germany.

Below: three divinities (bas-relief at House-steads, Northumberland).

However, the Roman geographer Pomponius Mela described the priestesses of the isle of Sein, off the shore of Brittany inhabited by the *Osismi*. They took a vow of perpetual virginity. The nine of them were known as *Gallizenae;* they were thought to be endowed with special talents, such as the ability to arouse the waves of the sea by their singing, to change into animals whenever they wished, to cure incurable sicknesses and to predict the future for the benefit of navigators who came to consult them.

This story seems, in fact, to be nothing more than a summary of some fable drawing heavily on the legend of Circe. One should note that the name of the druidess is not pronounced at any time. While we are inclined to accept Mela's account of the virgins of Sein only with considerable reservations, we do not find prophetesses called *dryads* in Gaul except during the 3rd century. One of them had predicted, to Alexander Severus, his imminent death—speaking Gaulish. Emperor Aurelian had consulted the Gaulish prophetesses, *Gallicanas Dryadas,* on the future of his offspring. One of these women had promised the empire to Diocletian (in fact, she was an innkeeper from Tongres). Even assuming that there were such creatures, the Gaulish druidesses, by this time, were merely fortune-tellers and nothing more.

There is no valid reason for applying the term *druidess* to the women referred to by Poseidonios as living without men on a

Three goddesses (High Rochester, Northumberland).

small island off the mouth of the Loire and engaging in the Bacchic cult. Once a year, their custom was to remove completely the roof of the temple of their god and to replace it in the same day. If one of them ever dropped the materials she was carrying during this operation, she was promptly torn to shreds by her companions.

Druidesses sometimes occurred among the Irish, as *ban drui,* or more often *ban file,* who, like the *file* were both soothsayers and poetesses at the same time.

The internal organisation of the corps of druids is rather important. According to Caesar, the druids merely had one chief who had absolute authority over them. When this chief died he was replaced by the worthiest among his fellows; if there was competition, the druids voted to decide who was the winner. Rivals for the top post were known, at times, to resolve the issue by force of arms!

In Ireland there were no supreme chiefs, hierarchies or druidic bodies. The druids acted alone, or in groups of two or three. They were married, and each lived at home. In a *Life of Saint Patrick* we learn that, one day, ten druids dressed in white united against the apostle of Ireland; nothing, however, indicates that these druids constituted any form of association.

Modern scholars have found the scant nature of our knowledge about the druids a distinct limitation. Late in the 17th century the huge stone monuments at Stone-henge and Avebury were attributed to the druids. The way in which the stones were aligned was explained by the cosmic serpent, whose coils they were thought to reproduce. The serpent was thought to be the symbol of the infinite Being, and the druids, it was claimed, had borrowed the idea from oriental mythologies.

Such fanciful archeological thinking, deriving from the English scholar Stukeley, soon made their way into France. In 1805, Cambry expounded, in his *Monuments Celtiques,* the druidic explanation of the megalithic monuments. The dolmens were assumed to be symbolic of treaties concluded between peoples, an emblem of union, stability and immutability. The respective positions of the celestial bodies and the relationship between that position and various points on earth were thought to be represented by stones arranged so as to give an idea of those positions in the heavens; it seemed logical to conclude therefrom that these symbolic monuments were in fact the first temples. This theory assumed that historical monuments were invariably copied by other peoples at later stages in history. The historian Henri Martin adopted the imaginative theories advanced by certain English scholars with more enthusiasm than critical reflexion.

*Assorted figures from
the Gundestrup Cauldron.*

90

7. GOVERNMENT AND SOCIETY. JUSTICE AND WAR.

Among the Celtic tribes, the form of government was either monarchical or oligarchical.

Late in the 4th century BC the chief of the coalition against the Marseillais was the minor Gaulish king Catumandus. Polybus mentions a king Magilos, who was originally from the plains watered by the River Po, and who challenged Hannibal's attempt to cross the Rhone. Later on, Hannibal found, among the Allobroges, two brothers who were contending for the royal throne, and he chose to lend his support to the elder of the two. At the beginning of the 1st century AD, the Arvernes were being governed by the king Bituitos, who was defeated in 121 by Q. Fabius Maximus.

About the time of Caesar's conquest of Gaul, there were no more kings left among the Celts, except for those of the *Nitiobroges* and the *Senones:* they were Teutomatus and Moritasgus. However, despite Caesar's protection, Cavarinus, who wanted to succeed Moritasgus, was rejected and then condemned to death by a popular assembly. In other tribes, kings who had been in power before the advent of Caesar were simply not replaced. Among the *Arverni,* one Celtillus was accused of seeking royal powers for himself and was executed. The Helvetian Orgetorix, charged with the same offense, was saved from his fate by a sudden, and no doubt voluntary, death. The royalty of Vercingetorix was only ephemeral; in fact,

Gold coin (1st century BC).

no sooner had he been named supreme chief of Gaul by his own people than he was being accused of treason. It seems, therefore, that royalty had become unpopular in Celtic Gaul.

The Bretons were governed by several kings and chiefs who lived in peace with one another most of the time, while the *Caledonii* had a democratic government, at least most of the time.

However, we know little of the attributes of royalty in either Gaul or the British Isles. Quite probably, the power of the kings was not very great, as they were almost certainly chosen by the people, and could be as easily deposed when the need arose. Ambiorix, king of the *Eburones*, told Caesar's envoys that the masses had more power over him than he had over them.

Caesar, in order to denote those in authority, used the term *magistratus*. Among the *Helvetii* the magistrates were the ones who summoned the farmers to defend the laws of the city by force of arms against Orgetorix. In some tribes there seems to have been a chief magistrate, *summus magistratus*. Among the *Aedui*, he was known as the *vergobretos;* he had the power of life and death, was appointed for one year only, could not leave the territory of the city, and was elected by the priests and the magistrates, in keeping with the conventions and legal forms of the time and place in question. The *Lexovii*, and perhaps also the *Santones,* had a magistrature of the same name. Any news of interest to the city also had to be forwarded first of all to the magistrates, who then concealed anything they thought unsuitable for public dissemination.

The influence of the magistrates was often opposed by men who took advantage of their elevated situation and their wealth to win the allegiance of the people. In this way, Orgetorix was able to avoid the effects of the judgment returned against him, thanks to the help of his clients. Similarly, Dumnorix enjoyed such authority amongst the *Aedui* that he met with no opposition when he demanded that the tolls and other taxes be levied; besides, he went everywhere surrounded by a strong force of cavalry paid for out of his own pocket. He was more influential than the magistrates. One wonders whether it was not through the distribution of funds that Luernios won over the favor of the masses and had himself made king.

At the beginning of each war the Gauls usually convened an armed assembly. Their law required that all the young adults attend this meeting armed: the man arriving last was tortured and put to death in public. Even when dealing with civic affairs, the Celts of the 3rd century BC used to attend their assemblies armed.

In the political assemblies Strabo says that they had a most peculiar custom. If a member of the audience were to interrupt the speaker or cause some commotion or other, the sergeant-at-arms would walk up to him and impose silence, with a threatening gesture; if the person committing a nuisance continued, the same official would repeat his order two or three times, and finally slice off a large chunk from the offending individual's *sagum,* thus rendering the remaining part unusable. Those present showed their approval of the proceedings by clanking their weapons instead of applauding.

Celtic assemblies, whether of one or of several cities, only met in grave circumstances, in order to reach decisions on joint action. There is no evidence of the existence of regularly held assemblies, at fixed intervals, and with well-defined attributions.

Caesar describes the *plebs* of Gaul as being in a state bordering on slavery, daring to do nothing on its own, and never being consulted about anything. It lived in a state of utter dependence on the authorities, though there do seem to have been various degrees of dependence. When Orgetorix was called before the tribunal to answer charges of high treason, he arrived with his entire *familia,* consisting of some ten thousand persons, including his clients and debtors, of whom there were many. This gives us an indication of at least three social classes: the slaves, who formed the greater part of the *familia,* in the broad sense of the term, the clients and the debtors. The clientèle of the Gaulish chiefs was often huge. The clientèle of Lucterius comprised the entire town of Uxellodunum.

In Ireland, as in Gaul, there were two

categories of vassals: the free vassals, or *soer-cheli*, and the non-free vassals, or *doer-cheli;* the word for vassal, *chele,* also meant "comrade". These vassals were bound to their overlord by a contract based on livestock. There were five social classes: kings, nobles, free landowners, free men without property, and non-free men.

Most probably, the boy that a Gaul would exchange for a measure of wine was a slave. There is no firm evidence that the children, of either sex, who waited on table at banquets were slaves. It is clear, however, that the Celts did bring back with them from their expeditions a great many slaves. Parthenios tells the story of a Milesian woman named Herippe who had been taken to Gaul as a slave, and whose husband tried to redeem her. The Celt, whom Aristodemus names Cavaras, was hospitable and generous, and would accept only a modest sum as ransom. The woman had her husband, whose name was Xanthos, admit that he had brought much more money than the amount he had offered to Cavaras; she then advised Cavaras to kill Xanthos, since she in any case detested him, and they would then be able to seize his fortune. When Xanthos, after paying the ransom, left with Herippe, Cavaras accompanied her; however, when the time came for them to set out on their return journey, he had Herippe stay with the intended victim, on the pretext that he wished to offer a sacrifice. Instead of killing Xanthos, he decapitated Herippe, and he

Gold coins; average size, one inch in diameter
(Paris, Cabinet des Médailles).

97

then told the husband of his wife's treachery and handed back the ransom.

For a brief summary of the structure of Celtic society, we could do far worse than turn to the historian Fustel de Coulages, who describes it thus: a great number of peasants and a tiny urban class, many men attached to the soil and few landowners; many servants and few masters; a plebeian class lacking utterly in status and importance, and a very powerful warrior aristocracy.

We know little of the judicial customs of the Celts. The authorities intervened only rarely, and most disputes were settled privately between the parties.

From the Irish epics we know the wording of the oath of Conchobhar, king of Ulster. "The sky is above us, the earth is be-

neath us, and the sea is all around. If the earth does not fall with a rain of stars on the face of the earth where we are encamped, if the earth does not shudder and break, if the sea, with its blue and grey solitude, does not sweep over the hairy forehead of life, I shall be victorious in battle and shall bring the cattle back to the stables and the women back to the houses!" In the 5th century BC, Loegaire, king of Ireland, made his oath to the sun and the moon, the water and the air, the day and the night, the sea and the land. As he did not keep his word, the earth swallowed him up, the sun burned him and the air abandoned him, so that he died.

One historian has discerned this same formula in the famous reply given by the Celts to Alexander, who had asked them

The Celtic citadel of Grianan of Aileach, Ireland.

what they feared most: "We fear only one thing, that the sky will fall in on us."

Certain disputes were decided among the Celts by duelling. Poseidonios reported having heard, in Gaul, that in ancient times, when hams were served at banquets, the strongest of the guests used to seize the leg for himself, and, if anyone challenged his right to it, both men would get up and fight it out to the death. The custom of reserving the best portions of food for the bravest men occurs in the Irish legend, where the hero's portion is the subject of one of the most stirring and vivid epics in the Ulster cycle: *The pork of Mac-Datho,* and goes to make up some important sections of the *Banquet of Bricriu.* In some instances, this might be a sort of judicial duel; often, however, it was merely a pas-

time. In Gaul, about the time of Poseidonios, dinner guests were in the habit of fighting among themselves after dinner; injuries, and even death, occurred from time to time.

When P. Cornelius Scipio Africanus declared his intention of staging gladiatorial combats in Carthagena, among the Celtiberians, in honor of his father and uncle, he was swamped with applicants from the local warrior population. Their number included some who had decided to resolve contentious issues by force of arms having failed to find a solution through discussion or negotiation. In Irish law, duelling was one of the accepted means whereby the parties to a legal dispute could settle their differences. If a contract had first been concluded with the consent of both parties,

Hunting scene: note the figure mounted on the bear and throwing a stone.

the family of the slain contender had no right to claim compensation for his death.

As for punishment for murder among the Gauls, Caesar devotes only one sentence to it: in cases of murder or crimes, the druids decided the issue and set the fines or punishments. Generally speaking the Celts used to prescribe a more severe punishment for the killing of a stranger than for that of a fellow-citizen, the penalties being, respectively, death and exile.

Those convicted of theft, highway-robbery or certain other crimes were burnt alive. Any Gaul caught hiding or stealing part of the booty obtained in war or any object deposited in a sacred place, was liable to be put to death after the most cruel tortures. According to Diodorus, such malefactors were kept for five years before being attached to stakes and burnt on huge bonfires. Fines or certain other light penalties were imposed on young people whose waist measurements were visibly excessive.

The authority of the Celtic state was most pre-eminent in military matters.

The writers of the ancient world depict the Celts as being constantly at war. When

Celto-Iberian buckle, with horseman (Archeological Museum, Madrid).

there was no possibility of war among themselves or against neighboring tribes, they offered their services in return for money to foreign kings. Scarcely a country in Europe did not see action involving Celtic mercenaries, who were to be found in virtually every armed conflict of their day. As early as 369 BC, an army sent by Denys the Elder to help the Spartans was partly composed of Celtic footsoldiers. In 274, Pyrrhus, king of Epirus, and Antigone Gonatas, king of Macedonia, both had Celtic mercenaries in their respective armies while they were at war with one another. In 238 BC Carthage came close to collapse as a result of a mutiny involving a Gaulish contingent headed by one Autaritos. In 262, the Carthaginians had recruited Celts for their Sicilian army; during the first two Punic Wars, there was a large Celtic element in the Carthaginian armies. There were a thousand Galatians in the army of Antigone, king of Macedonia, in 224; and Galatians cavalry fought in the army of another king of Macedonia, Philip V, in 218. Ptolemy Philadelphus had Gauls in his armies; indeed, he had four thousand of them slain for mutiny. Gauls

were also present in Cleopatra's guard.

In Gaul, with the exception of the druids, all free men were obliged to do their military service. As we have seen, all men capable of bearing arms were summoned at the beginning of a war.

The military command seems to have been different from the civil authority. According to Strabo, chiefs were chosen to serve for one year; similarly, for a war, a single general was elected by the multitude.

It often happened that a single chief commanded the forces of various peoples. Galba, king of the *Sessiones,* was in command of the *Belgii,* with whom he was in coalition. Cassivellaunus was chosen a commander-in-chief by tribes from the south of the British Isles, though he had previously spent much of his time at war with them. Ambiorix and Camulogenus commanded coalitions of Gaulish tribes.

In the year 61, Boudicca, commanding the Breton army, recalled the tradition whereby the Celts went into battle led by a woman. A number of texts of ancient Irish laws seem to imply that daughters who, having no brothers, inherited their parent's possessions, were obliged to undergo military service. This obligation was abolished in the 7th century.

The Celts who invaded Greece had two mounted servants for each member of the cavalry. During the battle, they stayed in the background, stepping forward only if their master should fall in action; if he was

wounded, one would take him back to camp, while the other would take his place in action; if he were to be unhorsed, one of his aides would recover his horse and help him to mount it. The Gauls of Illyria had a similar arrangement. Each soldier on horseback was accompanied by a foot-soldier who would replace him if he was thrown from his horse in battle. According to Caesar, the Germanic tribes of Ariovista had similar tactics; in fact, their infantry were so fleet of foot that, by hanging on to the horse's mane, they could keep up with the cavalry.

In the earliest times for which records exist the Gauls of Italy had cavalry and also warriors riding on chariots. At the battle of Sentinum, in 295 BC, some thousand chariots were in action at the same time. At the battle of Telamon, seventy years later, there were twenty thousand warriors, either on horseback or on chariots. In 222 King Virdomarus rode into battle at Clastidium hurling spears from a fast-moving chariot. The Gauls of Italy seem to have abandoned the use of chariots in war at an early date.

In 121, the king of the *Arvernes*, Bituitos, fought in a battle at the confluence of the Isère and the Rhône riding a silver-clad chariot. By the time Caesar appeared on the scene, however, there seem to have been no war chariots left in the Gaulish armies. He was to find two-wheeled war chariots for the first time in the British Isles.

In Champagne, skeletons of warriors have been found, buried inside their chariots, with iron wheel-rims and bronze axles nearby. These graves date from before the conquest of Gaul, and must have belonged to the peoples which preceded the *Belgi* of Caesar's time. In Britain, remains of the iron-work of war-chariots have been found in burial mounds in Yorkshire.

From the epic literature of Ireland it is clear that the Irish were fighting in chariots as late as the early centuries of the Christian era. Mounted warriors occur only rarely in the oldest texts of the Ulster cycle; mounted combat replaces the use of chariots in the cycle of Leinster. The Irish war-chariot had two men in it: a warrior on the left, and the driver on the right. This was a two-wheeled chariot drawn by two horses. There is only one instance of a chariot armed with scythe-blades: this was the *cath-charpat-serda* of the heroes of Ulster, Cuchulainn. It was equipped with iron spikes, fine blades, teeth, and had axles which were positively bristling with jagged edges.

In the epic literature of Ireland there are several examples of one-man battles fought on behalf of whole armies. The most famous of these is contained in the epic entitled the *Seizure of the Cows of Cualnge*. While the warriors of Ulster were reduced to impotence as a result of a curse which had been cast on them, Cuchulainn withstood the onslaught of the invading armies of Connacht all on his own. A deal

Horseman carrying a severed head, Entremont.

was proposed whereby a warrior would be sent each morning to fight a duel with him, and, during this time, Connacht's army would not press its advance. In this way, Cuchulainn fought eleven warriors; after the seventh he took a rest for three days and nights; the eleventh combat lasted three whole days.

The Gaulish fortresses which Caesar called *oppida* occupied quite a vast area: Murcens extended over 370 acres, Bibractium 340, Besançon 370, Alisa 240, and Gergovia 170. They were situated in places having their own natural fortifications:

Avaricum was surrounded by marshes and rivers, while Gergovia and Alisia were on the top of a mountain. The walls, built in the Gaulish manner, were between 15 and 30 feet thick. At Noviodunum they were high, and looked over a wide ditch. Towers made of wood covered with leather had been erected on the walls at Avaricum.

When under siege the Gauls would take to the towers and ramparts, whence they would hurl down on the enemy below a variety of burning objects, such as wood, torches, pitch, soot, etc. At Gergovia and Alesia they had built a tall stone wall,

made of huge boulders, on top of the hill on which their fortress was situated.

Some particular war-cries had a special significance. Besides the cry they uttered on moving into the attack, there was also a victory cry, and another which signalled their intention to negotiate. In order to ensure that their allies recognized them, the Gauls had a peace sign—a bare right shoulder.

All the details which it has proved possible to collect about the military customs of the Celts show us that the Celtic state was organized with war in mind: wars of invasion and conquest, and wars of defense against invaders.

This was virtually the only sphere in which the collective power of the citizens really made itself felt; in matters such as relations between individuals and religious beliefs and institutions it was apparently inactive.

Left: lance, Tène period
(Luxembourg State Museum).
Right: Gaulish warrior (Musée
de l'Armée, Paris).

8. THE CELTIC EXPANSION.

Excavations at the Enserunde Oppidum, a Klto-Ligurian site in the department of Héraut, France.

Before the end of the 6th century BC there is no reference to any country occupied by the Celts. Three fragments of the *Description of the Earth* by Hecatea of Milet (540–475), kept intact by Stephen of Byzantium, the author of a geographical dictionary (late 5th century AD) which was revised in the 6th century by Hermalaos, contain the name *Celtic.* The first fragment mentions Narbonne, a Celtic trading center and town; the second, Massalia; and the third names Nyrax, a Celtic town, the exact location of which is unknown. In the 6th century the Ligurians occupied the Mediterranean coasts between the Alps and the mouth of the Rhone.

Herodotus, in two passages written between 445 and 432, tells us that the Istros (Danube) was a river whose sources lay in Celtic territory, near the town of Pyrene. The Celts lived beyond the Pillars of Hercules, and were the neighbors of the *Cynesii (Cynetes)* the last people of Europe as one went east. The land of the *Cynetes* was in the south of what is now Portugal. It seems that, whether or not the term Pyrene denotes the Pyrenees, where ancient geographers had situated the source of the Danube, Herodotus was convinced that the territory of the Celts extended into a part of the Iberian peninsula. In the records of his travels left by the Carthaginian Himilcon, the Celts are only mentioned in connection with an uninhabited area to the north of Cape

Oestrymnis, and from which the Ligurians were expelled by the Celts. The island he named *sacra insula,* or sacred island was inhabited by the *Hierni,* and was next to the island of the *Albiones.* From these names one can easily infer that he was talking about the British Isles.

According to Arrian, in the time of Xenophon, the peoples of western Europe were relatively unknown. However, Xenophon does mention the Celtic mercenaries sent as reinforcements by Denys of Syracuse to the Lacedemonians.

Aristotle situated the mountain of Pyrene towards the western equinoctial, in Celtica. He also referred to the cold climate of the land of the Celts, above the Iberias. According to him, the Rhone went underground in Ligystica (it actually occurs upstream from Bellegarde). He also mentions the taking of Rome by the Celts.

About the year 350, Theopompus mentions the most remote of all the Celtic towns: *Drilonios.* We cannot be sure of its exact location. He describes the Celts at war with the *Vardii,* an Illyrian people, and also mentions the taking of Rome by the Celts.

An account of a long journey made by Scylax of Caryanda, and written about 335, refers only to the Greek settlers and the Ligurians as inhabiting the Mediterranean coast between the Pyrenees and Italy. The Celts who had remained after the invasion occupied a narrow strip of land on the eastern coast of Italy, as far as Adria.

After the Celts came the Venetes, through whose territory flowed the Eridan (Po).

Ephorus is known to the modern reader only through Strabo and Cosmas Indicopleustes (6th century AD). In his opinion the Celts were one of the peoples occupying the very end of the world; their country, which was situated in the west, and which extended all the way from the winter to the summer sunset, was smaller than the territory of the Ethiopians and the Scythians. The losses they suffered on account of the water greatly exceeded their losses in war: the waves would come in and sweep over their houses, which would then have to be rebuilt. The Celts were in control of the greater part of the Iberian peninsula as far as Gadeira (Cadiz).

These vague notions about the regions occupied by the Celts would have been much enhanced by the full record of the journey of exploration made by Pytheas in western Europe about 320–310, most of which has unfortunately been lost. The few fragments reproduced by Strabo, dealing with the Celtic possessions, do not add much to our knowledge. According to Pytheas, *Cantion* (Kent) was several days' by boat from Celtica.

Ptolemy, son of Lagos, of one Alexander's lieutenants related the celebrated interview which took place between Alexander and the Celts of the Adriatic, in 335 BC, during which, when asked what they feared most, they replied: "There is one thing that we fear more than anything else

in the world—it is that the sky might fall in on us; but we place the friendship of a man such as you above all else."

Jerome of Cardia, who continued Ptolemy's history of Alexander, related the Celtic invasion in Greece; indeed, his work on this subject is doubtless the source used by Diodorus and Pausanias.

The historian Timea (352–356) was familiar with the Celts who inhabited the Atlantic coast; he explained the rise and fall of the tides by the effect of the rivers which flow into the Atlantic from the mountains in the territory of the Celts. This author is doubtless the source of the treatise *Of certain singular wonders*, attributed to Aristotle, and of works by Apollonios of Rhodes.

Callimachus, the librarian of Alexandria under Ptolemy II (283–247) wrote a hymn about the invasion of Greece by the Celts, the last-born of the Titans, who had come from the very ends of the Western world.

Eratosthenes, who held the same post under Ptolemy III (247–222), thought that the Galatians occupied the western part of Europe as far as Gadeira, doubtless basing his views of those of Ephorus. However, in his description of Iberia, he made no further reference to the Galatians.

In the *Argonautics* of Apollonios of Rhodes (3rd century BC) the Argonauts went up the Rhone and found themselves in the midst of the stormy lakes which cov-

Bridge, from the Celtic period, over the River Barle, at Tarr-Steps, Somerset.

117

The statuette known as the "Bouray god" (Museum of Saint-Germain-en-Laye).

ered vast areas in the territory of the Celts; then, after reaching the seashore, they passed through the numerous tribes of Celts and Ligyians.

The first Roman historian, Q. Fabius Pictor, born in 254 BC, wrote an account of the war between the Romans and the *Gaesati,* a people from Gaul.

In this way, in the 2nd century BC, at a time when a reliable and well-informed historian, Polybus, described the earliest relations between the Celts and the Romans, the information which we find in the historians and geographers of antiquity about the lands occupied by the Celts is scant indeed. We know that the Celts had settled near the Ligurians: from Rimini to Ancona, on the Adriatic coast; in Illyria, along the banks of the Danube; near the lakes of present-day Switzerland and the sources of the Rhone, the Po and the Danube; and, finally, on the coasts of Spain.

Polybus was particularly familiar with the Celts of Italy. According to him, the Celts living near the Tyrrhenes (Etruscans), were so attracted by the beauty and fertility of the plain of the Po that they swept in, on some flimsy pretext, and dislodged them from the area entirely. He gives the names of some of the Celtic tribes which then settled in the Cisalpine area. They were the *Lai (Laevi),* the *Lebecii,* the *Isombres (Insubres),* the *Gonomani (Cenomani),* the *Ananes (Anares* or *Anamares),* the *Boii,* the *Lingones* and the *Senones.* After the fall of Rome, the Celts

were obliged to come to terms with the Romans as a result of an invasion of their territory by the Venetes.

As for the Transalpine Gauls, who belonged to the same race as the Cisalpines, they occupied, according to Polybus, the part of the Alps facing the Rhone, and the north. Between the Alps and the Rhone were the Galatians, also known as the *Gaesati.* On his way from Spain to Italy Hannibal found Celts living between the Pyrenees and the Rhone and then beyond the Rhone. The northern part of the Rhone valley was occupied by the *Ardyes* Celts *(Aedui?).* Between the Narbonne area and the Pyrenees, the population consisted virtually entirely of Celts.

Again according to Polybus, the countries situated on the Ocean coast had only been recently discovered, and still lacked a common name: "They are inhabited by large numbers of barbarians . . . the entire area between Narbonne and the Tanais (Don) is quite unknown. Possibly, active research might shed some light on it; but I must say that those who write or talk about these areas are simply inventing fables, and know as little about them as we do." In the opinion of Polybus, the descriptions written by Pytheas as a result of his travels were of no value whatsoever. Unfortunately, the chapters which Polybus said he was going to write about the barbarians of the Ocean coast have been lost.

In Spain, Polybus studied certain Celtic

119

peoples: he described the *Celtici* as neighbors of the *Turdetani,* and wrote accounts of the wars between the Celtiberians and the Romans. The territory of the Celtiberians extended from Sagonta (Murviedro) to the sources of the Anas (Guadiana) and the Baetis (Guadalquivir); it was occupied by the *Vaccaei* in the Duero basin, the *Aravacae (Arevaci)* whose region included the famous town of Numantium, the *Belli* and the *Titti.*

Polybus makes only passing reference to the Celtic settlements in the Balkans. He does mention the defeat inflicted on Ptolemy Keraunos, king of Macedonia, in 281, by the Galatians, the resistance of the Etolians against the Galatians under Brennos, in 279, and the desctruction of part of the Galatian army during the expedition to Delphi. After this disaster the Galatians dispersed, some of them turning towards Thrace, where they founded a state whose capital was Tyle and to which the Byzantine Greeks paid tribute. The first king of this state was Comontorios, and the last, Cavaros. The Thracians destroyed this Gaulish kingdom during the 3rd century BC. Other parts of the former Galatian army settled in Asia Minor: these were the *Tolistobogii,* the *Tectosages* and the *Trocmi.* Other Gaulish peoples were summoned into Asia Minor as mercenaries. In 220 BC, there were *Tectosages* serving in the army of Antiochus III, king of Syria. Some of the Aigosages who had served under Attala I, king of Pergamo,

founded an independent state on the Hellespont, at Troad; this state was destroyed in 216 by Prusias, king of Bithynia.

The *Chronicles* of Apollodorus (2nd century BC), in two fragments kept by Stephen of Byzantium, mention the *Aidusii,* the *Aedui* who were Roman allies in an area near Celtic Gaul, and the *Arverni,* who were the most warlike branch of the Galatians.

The passages from Poseidonios which have been quoted in historical works tell us nothing about the areas occupied by the Celts.

A travel account attributed to Scymnus of Chio described the area between Tartessos and the sea of Sardinia as the land of the Celts, the greatest nation in the West.

Artemidoris of Ephesus wrote an eleven-volume treatise on geography, early in the 1st century BC, which was heavily used by Strabo in his writings.

The first Latin historians left very little information about the Celts. Cato mentions the *Lepontii* (near Domodossola) and the *Salassi* (near Aosta). He also observes that the *Cenomani* (from near Bergamo and Trent) were a branch of the Volcae, and that the *Boii* were divided into one hundred and twelve tribes. Sempronius Asellio mentions the town of Noreia as being in Gaul; in fact, it is the modern Neumark, in Styria.

It was not until Julius Caesar that fuller information on the Celts of Gaul and the

British Isles was recorded. Cicero, though giving the names of certain Gaulish peoples such as the *Allobroges,* the *Volcae* and the *Ruteni,* was nonetheless able to say: "Our general, our troops and our arms have ranged far and wide through regions and nations of which nothing had been written and nothing was known. Previously, we had occupied only a path through Gaul, the rest of which was in the hands of peoples which were either the enemies of the empire, or were unreliable, unknown, or at least fierce, barbaric and warlike."

"The campaigns of Caesar has revealed successively for us all the parts of Gaul—the east, where the *Aedui* live, the north-east occupied by the Belgian peoples the north-west, where the Armorican confederation was formed, and the center, where the supreme struggle being waged by Vercingetorix for the independence of Gaul is taking place. For the first time, a Roman army has penetrated into the British Isles, the existence of which was barely known. In this way, a large part of the Celtic world became revealed to the Romans within the space of a few years. Caesar's expeditions beyond the Rhine having brought him into contact only with Germanic peoples, it seemed logical that, henceforth, Gaul should be considered as the center of Celtic power and the cradle of the Celtic race. In Caesar's own words: "There was a time when the Gauls, being of superior valor to the Germanic tribes,

Above: a Gaul on his knees. Right: bronze figurine, apparently the Celtic god Tarani.

used to carry the war into their territory and dispatch settlers beyond the Rhine simply because they had too large a population, with insufficient land to feed it. In this way, the *Volcae Tectosages* seized the most fertile land of Germania, near the Hercynian forest. They remain there to this day, and enjoy a great reputation for justice and valor.''

Authors writing later than Caesar, when they confine themselves to the reproduction of earlier evidence, have sometimes left us valuable information about the size of the ancient Celtic empire, the most interesting in this respect being Livy. Before giving his account of the defeat of the Romans by the Gauls, Livy wrote in some detail about Gaulish immigration into Italy. At the time when Rome was ruled by Tarquin the Elder, sovereign power among the Celts, who accounted for one third of the whole of Gaul, was in the hands of the *Bituriges*. The king in question was Ambigatus, who wielded immense power, by virtue both of his own merits and of those of his people; under his rule, Gaul became so abundant in men and in the fruits of the earth that it was difficult for one king to govern so large a mass. Feeling the advance of age, and wishing to rid his kingdom of surplus manpower, he decided to send Bellovesus and Sigovesus, his sister's sons, both of them dynamic young men, to settle wherever the gods chose to suggest through signs and omens from on high. They were to raise a force of such strength that no na-

Prisoner and warrior (Triumphal Arch and Museum of Nîmes).

tion would ever be able to repel such new-comers. As it happened, Sigovesus got the Hercynian forest, while the gods gave Bellovesus a much more superb fate—Italy. Having raised a large army from among tribes such as the *Bituriges, Arverni, Aedui, Senones,* etc., with a considerable force of cavalry apart from his foot-soldiers, he entered the territory of the *Tricastini.* The Gauls also helped, the Phocaeans become established at Marseille; then they crossed the Alps via the territory of the *Taurini,* and, having routed the *Tusci* near the site of modern Tessin, they settled in the area known in those days as Insubria.

According to this account, the Celtic invasion of Italy was contemporary with Tarquin the Elder (616–578 BC) and the foundation of Marseille (600 BC). However, when Livy describes the first en-counter between Romans and Gauls, in 390 BC, it seems that this was the first time that the barbarians had ever appeared in Italy and met the Romans. There is therefore a discrepancy between the two texts. Moreover, Polybus tells us that the Tyrrhenians (Etruscans) were the masters of the plain of the Po during the period in which they were in control of the neighboring areas of Nole and Capua. It was only under the consulate of M. Genucius and C. Curtius, in 445 BC, that the *Campani* rebelled, while it was not until 424 BC that they seized the town of Capua from the Etruscans. According to Polybus, the Gauls did not seize Rome, which they occupied fully except for the Capitol, until 19 years after the battle of Aigos Potamos (405), 16 years before the battle of Leuctres (371), at the time when the Lacede-

monians concluded the Treaty of Antalcidas (387–386) and when Denys, having triumphed over the Greeks of Italy, had laid siege to Rhegium. The relationship between these four dates give us 387–386 BC as the year in which Rome fell. Roman chronology would give the year 390 BC as the period of the military tribunes during which the battle of Allia was fought. The taking of Rome by the Gauls thus occurred about three years after the Celtic invasion of Italy, if one follows Polybus and one of Livy's texts, and almost two hundred years afterwards, if one takes Livy's first text as authentic. As we shall see, Appian gives the 97th Olympiad (392–389) as the date of the Gaulish invasion of Italy.

The account of the invasion given by Bellovesus raises another question, this time geographical in nature. In the words of Livy, this invasion took place *per Taurinos saltusque Juliae Alpis*. However, the *Taurini* lived in the vicinity of Turin, in north-west Italy, and the *Julia Alpis* is now known as the Birnbaumerwald, a mountain in north-east Italy. One can hardly claim that the Celts penetrated into the Cisalpine area from either end of the Alps. Yet the manuscripts all give *iuliae,* with the exception of the *Harleianus I* text, where the word is *juria.* Various scholars, baffled by this contradiction, have tried in vain to correct *iuliae* to *Liguriae, Duriae, inuias* or *inuios;* yet they have never managed to explain why simple forms such as *inuias, inuios, Liguriae* and *Duriae* could have

Left: small plate from a harness. Right:
assorted jewels (Archeological Museum
of Madrid).

126

Left: Celtiberian figure (terra cotta).—Right: One of the figures from the Mainz Column, a fine specimen of Gallo-Roman art.

129

changed to *iuriae,* which isn't even Latin. Neither have they explained why most manuscripts have chosen the word *iuliae.*

One is entitled to wonder, assuming that the reading of the manuscripts is correct, if Livy might not have combined two different traditions, whereby the Gauls came, respectively, from the north-west and the north-east of Italy. What were Livy's sources on this point? He must surely have drawn on the treatise of geography and the three-volume chronicle of Cornelius Nepos. Unfortunately only fragments of these works have survived intact, and those are irrelevant to the subject we are considering.

It would be much easier to admit that there had been some confusion, due either to a historian or to a scribe, between *Taurini* and *Taurisci,* since the latter was the name of the tribe which had settled precisely in the *Julia Alpis.*

Diodorus of Sicily wrote that the British Isles, before Caesar's time, had never been invaded by foreign forces. Gaul, on the other hand, had been visited by Herakles, who had a son named Galates, by the king's daughter. The Iberians and the Celts fought for a long time to achieve supremacy in Spain, but they eventually merged. At the time of the siege of Rhegium by Denys the Elder (388–387), the Celts living beyond the Alps crossed the mountains and took control, with powerful forces, of the area situated between the Apennines and the Alps, having first expelled the Tyrrhenians who had been living there.

The summary of Timogenes by Ammian Marcellinus contains some curious details about the early history of the Celts. According to certain traditions, the Celts were aboriginals in Gaul, though the druids maintained that tribes from the furthest islands and from across the Rhine soon came to join the original population. In the opinion of others, the territory next to the Ocean was inhabited by the Dorians who had followed Herakles.

Cornelius Nepos maintained that the Etruscan town of Melpum was destroyed by the *Boii,* the *Insubres* and the *Senones* the same day that Veies was seized from the Etruscans.

Denys of Halicarnassus has the following to say about Celtica: "Celtica is situated in the western part of Europe, between the boreal pole and the equinox of the setting sun. It is in the form of a tetragon; in the east it touches the Alps, which are the highest mountains in Europe; in the south and south-east it reaches the Pyrenees; while in the west its limits are the seas beyond the Pillars of Hercules. The Scythian and Thracian races live in the north and in the region of the Danube, the biggest river in the region, which flows from its source in the Alps across the entire northern continent and empties into the Pontus Euxinus (Black Sea). Celtica is so big that it can be said to comprise almost one quarter of Europe. It is watered by numerous rivers; it is fertile, with abundant

crops and large amounts of livestock grazing on its pastures. It is divided into two equal parts by the Rhine, which, after the Danube, seems to be the greatest of the rivers of Europe. The area on this side of the Rhine, towards the territory of the Scythians and the Thracians, is called Germania. It reaches as far as the Hercynian forest and the Rhipean mountains. The other part, which extends as far south as the Pyrenees and which surrounds the Galatian Gulf, is named Galatia, after the name of the sea. The Greeks know this whole territory, with both its parts, by the name Celtica."

Denys clearly combined Gaul and Germany in his *Celtica*. According to him, the Celtic invasion of Italy was caused by an Etruscan, Arruns, who, seeking to avenge the seduction of his wife by Lucumon, persuaded the Gauls from beyond the Alps to go and settle in Italy. He drove chariots loaded with wine, oil and figs into their territory; they became so quickly accustomed to these good things that they were determined to leave as soon as possible for the country where they could be grown.

Trogus Pompeius, as abridged by Justinian, describes the Gaulish invasions in these terms: "The Gauls, finding that they could no longer feed their population, so vast had it become, had sent three hundred thousand of their number to seek a new place to live in foreign lands. Some of them

131

stopped in Italy, capturing and burning Rome in the process; others, guided by the flight of certain birds, entered Illyria, where, having first massacred the barbarians living there, they settled at Pannonia. This rough, bold and warlike people were the first, after Hercules, to cross the invincible summits of the Alps and the places which, on account of the cold, were totally forbidding to man. Having vanquished the Pannonians, they spent many years fighting their neighbors. Emboldened by their success they divided into two armies, one of which took Greece, while the other took Macedonia, destroying everything by the sword as they went." In another text, Justinian attributes the invasion of Italy by the Gauls to internecine strife and a state of perpetual anarchy, and observes that the result of this invasion was the expulsion of the Etruscans. His treatment of the Gaulish invasion of Italy is so close, in both language and thinking, to Livy's text that both of them must be based on the same source.

In the opinion of Strabo, the Celts of Italy came from the country beyond the Alps. Celtic elements had mingled with the Germanic, Illyrian and Thracian populations of the area south of the Istros. The *Autariatae,* the largest and bravest people of Illyria, were first subjugated by the *Scordisci,* a Celtic people, and later by the Romans, whose onslaught also overcame the *Scordisci,* who had long prevailed in the area. After years of wandering, the Gala-

tians occupied Asia Minor and made incursions into territories under the suzerainty of the kings of Pergamo and Bithynia.

Plutarch attributes the invasion to excess of population and a lack of resources in Celtica. The Gauls, numbering hundred of thousands of strong young men, with women and children, divided into two groups, one of which crossed the Rhipean mountains, spread out towards the northern ocean and occupied the extremities of Europe, while the others, who had settled between the Pyrenees and the Alps, lived for many years near the *Sennones* and the *Celtorii.* It was not until later, when they had tasted Italian wine, that they invaded the country which produced such a superb drink.

According to Plorus, the *Sennones* swept out of the furthest corners of the ocean coast, ravaged many of the regions in their path, and settled between the Alps and the Po, whence they spread out throughout Italy. The Gallogreeks (Galatians of Asia) are the remnants of the Gauls, who, under the leadership of Brennus, had devastated Greece.

Denys the Periegetes placed the Celts after the Iberians and the Pyrenees, near the sources of the Eridan. The children of the Celts, sitting beneath the poplars, along the banks of this splendid river, used to collect the tears of amber.

In Books IV and VI of Appian's *Roman History,* an account is given of the first migrations of the Celts. Between 392 and 389 BC, a large proportion of the Celts living near the Rhine began to look for somewhere else to live, as their own territory could not support their large numbers. They crossed the Alps and attacked the inhabitants of Clusium. Appian thought that the Celts had originally crossed the Pyrenees and dwelt together with the earliest inhabitants of the peninsula—whence the name *Celtiberians*.

Pausanias describes the Celtic invasions of Greece, which he divides into three major expeditions. The first was a sort of raid into Thrace; the Celts did not dare to go any further, as they recognized that they were no match for the Greeks. The second was a simultaneous invasion of Thrace, Peonia, Macedonia and Illyria. After defeating the Macedonians, the Celts went back home. The third began with the invasion of Macedonia, whence the Celts pressed on towards central Greece, through Thessaly. After vain attempts to penetrate into Greece by the Sperchios and the Oeta, they split up into two separate armies, one of which went north, invaded Etolia and was driven back by the Etolians. The other went around the Thermopyleans and reached Delphi, where a coalition of Greek forces inflicted heavy casualties on them. The Celts retreated towards the Sperchios, but were attacked by the Thessalians; none of them returned home. As for the country which the Celts originally set out from, Pausanias says

nothing; he simply uses the phrase "the barbarians of the ocean" to describe them; he also says that the Galatians lived in the furthest corners of Europe, near a vast sea, the outer limits of which were inaccessible to any ships. This sea had a tide, breakers and monsters which were quite unlike those found in other seas. Their territory was located, according to him, near the Eridan, on whose banks it was thought that the daughters of the Sun used to lament the fate of Phaeton, their brother.

How much of this abundant, and yet often imprecise information provided by the Latin and Greek authors about the ancient Celts should one accept at face value? Principally, the notion that Celtic domination was not limited to Transalpine and Cisalpine Gaul and to Celtiberia, but that the Celts also settled in north-west and central Europe. Moreover, the historians of antiquity have all described Celtic migrations to Spain, Italy, Germany, the British Isles, Thrace and Asia Minor. We must now consider whether the archeological and linguistic evidence tallies with the findings of historians.

The Celts have left evidence of their presence in all regions where they settled. Some of these are anonymous, like the objects found in the graves of Austria and eastern France; others are of a more linguistic nature—names of places and persons preserved in texts and inscriptions.

The Halstatt civilization, in the opinion of Hoernes, consisted of two zones, one in

the south, made up of Carniola, southern Styria, Carinthia and the Tyrol, where the influence of the Illyrians was predominant; and the other in the north, covering Lower and Upper Austria, western Hungary, Bohemia and Moravia, Upper Bavaria, the Upper Palatinate, the Duchy of Baden, Wurtemberg, Hesse, Alsace, eastern, central and south-west Gaul. It extends only slightly into nothern Italy, north and west Gaul and the British Isles. So far, it has not been found at all in the Iberian peninsula.

The Tène civilization extends over a much vaster area. It occurs in Gaul, particularly in the *oppida*, the graveyards of Champagne, the British Isles, northern Italy, Bosnia, Bohemia, Germany and even in southern Scandinavia.

Neither of these two civilizations was exclusively limited to the areas which historians have deemed to be Celtic. Apart from anything else, the two zones do not coincide exactly. When we compare their extent in an area as unquestionably Celtic as Gaul it becomes evident that they are juxtaposed rather than intermingled. For example, the Halstatt civilization has been observed in Burgundy, Franche-Comté, the Pyrenees, the Tarn and Berry; and the Tène civilization has been recorded in Champagne, Bas-Dauphiné, Forez, Ardèche, the *oppida* of Bibractium, Alesia, Murcens (Lot) and others of lesser importance.

A comparison of historical and archeological data shows that they do not tally

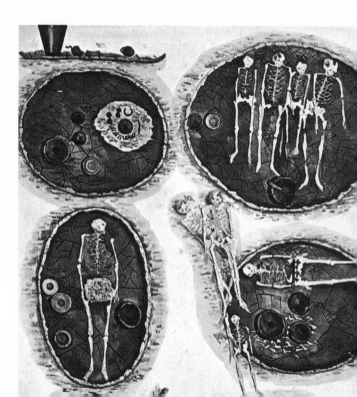

136

Site and remains of the burial ground
of Halstatt, in the Salzkammergut.

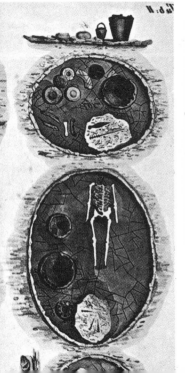

The site and remains of Beaghmore, Ireland.

completely. The Halstatt civilization seems earlier than the period for which we have precise and detailed information about the migrations of the Celts. The Tène civilization comprises three centuries of the history of the Celts, from the taking of Rome until Caesar's conquest of Gaul. In detail, however, the findings of archeology do not always concur with what we know historically about the Celts.

The first period of the Tène civilization, from the 4th to the 3rd centuries, is the period to which the Champagne graves belong. Yet the men whose remains were buried there were not the *Belgi*, as we know them from history. First of all, they buried their dead; they had war chariots; they did not use coins; they used coral; and their iron swords were of an older type than the Gaulish swords discovered at Alesia.

The second period, from the 3rd to the end of the 2nd centuries, to which the Tène site itself belongs, seems to be from a period when the *Helvetii* had not yet entered the territory they occupied at the time of Caesar's conquest.

The third period, covering the first century, and which is represented by the *oppida* of Gaul, is the only one in respect of which the results of archeology and history can be made to coincide.

The findings of archeology tell us two important things: of the two civilizations with which the Celts are commonly associated, one seems to have emanated from central Europe, whence it spread some dis-

139

tance east and west; the other may well
have originated in north-east Gaul, from
where it spread throughout western, eastern and northern Europe.

Two specimens of the Celtic cross, one of which bears a swastika (Ireland).

Credits: Bord Failte: 22, Griffin: 116, Hurault: 64b, Muller: 58, 63, 67, 81, 84, 91, 122, 129, 137, N.D.: 65, V. Rossi/Ricciarini: 17, 73, 138, S.E.F.: 6, 9, 20, 23, 26, 30, 32, 35, 39b, 41, 53, 56, 71, 108, 109, 121, 127, 128, Unedi: 8, 10, 11, 12, 13, 18, 24b, 33, 40, 44, 47, 48, 69, 72, 92, 97, 101, 102, 106, 107b, 113, 114, 125, 132, 135, 144, Viollet: End-papers 2, 5, 14, 21, 27, 42a, 42b, 43, 52, 66, 74, 76, 77, 98, 103, 110, 118, 141.